Dear Itsie

A Memoir of Survival

by

Phillip William

Dorrance Publishing Co
585 Alpha Drive
Suite 103
Pittsburgh, PA 15238
Visit our website at *www.dorrancebookstore.com*

ISBN: 978-1-6495-7063-5
eISBN: 978-1-6495-7003-1

Dear Itsie

Dear Itsie,

I'm writing this for you. I hope that it will help you understand who I am and how things that have happened in my life shaped my behavior and many of the decisions that I made. You are a beautiful, talented, wonderful young woman, and I am so very proud to be your father. I love you very much and I understand and accept that you are struggling to come to terms with who I am and how we can have the happy and healthy relationship that we both want. You've been through an awful lot in your seventeen years but you'll get through all of this, I promise.

I can only imagine how confusing and painful it must be to try and make sense out of the situation you have with me. Your mother and I were married for seventeen years; we had four children together, and now for the first time in my life, I'm in love, with Tom.

Believe it or not I can relate to some of what you're experiencing. Living in fear that other people are going to figure out the truth about you is something I know very well. I know it's why you don't have your friends over, why you don't want a graduation party; you have a secret. So I don't think that you and I are terribly different in that way—you are going to great lengths to make sure everything appears normal about you and your family. So did I, all of my childhood and most of my adult years.

Having a gay parent must surely present its own challenges for any child growing up today, but having a gay father who was married for almost two decades to your mother must create an enormous amount of questioning and uncertainty. You have every right to distrust what I say and what I do; in your mind, I lived a lie, or at least I did not live an authentic life. Therefore, since you believe me to be capable of presenting to the world what I think they want to see and not who I am, how do you know when it's real?

That is why I am writing this to you and for all of my children. So that you will know what is real; most of what you will read about I have never shared with anyone but I think it is important that I share it with all of you. This is difficult for me, I have kept secrets all my life. From a very early age I never wanted anyone to know what was really happening to me. Even as an adult I feared that if anyone knew who I really was, or what happened in my family, they wouldn't want to have any kind of relationship with me at all. But you deserve the truth and I would do anything, no matter how difficult, to help you get through this. I will never give up fighting for us. From my perspective, this is the first time in my life everyone is seeing me for who I am. So I have written this so that you and your brother and sisters can know the truth and try and make sense out of what is a very complicated and confusing situation for all of you.

You said that you don't know me, I hope after reading this you feel that you know me very well, and even if you don't agree with the choices I made or the things that I've done, I think you'll understand me. I warn you that you won't like everything that you're going to learn but given how I lived my life for the first four decades, I think we have to start at the beginning.

I will try to help you understand why I never believed that I lied to your mother, I loved her in the only way I had ever experienced loving another person, and I was as honest with her as I was with myself. Denial is a very powerful tool and I used that to try and convince myself, as much as everyone else, that I was normal. And all of my life, above all else, I wanted to be "normal." I wanted desperately to have what I thought everyone else had: a normal, happy life. In that way we are both very much alike, I'm sure part of your anxiety is having friends or kids at school find out the truth about your father. It isn't "normal" or at least it isn't typical. So maybe you can understand how hard I tried to fit in, to be someone people would like and accept.

As you read this please keep in mind that I am not offering any of the things that happen to me in my life as excuses for actions and behaviors that you find unacceptable. I take full responsibility for all that I have done and mistakes that I've made, but it's important to me that you do know who I am. I never want to see you or any of my children in any pain, and the thought that I am the cause of any suffering tears at my heart.

I can't make up for what's happened to you and I can't take the away the pain that you suffered but I can make amends and I can share my story with you and hopefully provide you with some of the answers that you seek.

I love you now and forever,

Dad

Prelude

Nor-mal (adjective) ['no;rml] Conforming to a standard; usual, typical, ordinary.

Normal. All my life, as far back as I can remember, that's all I wanted. In order for you to understand what motivated me and shaped many, if not most, of my decisions as an adult, then you must start there.

And in order to understand how and why that became not just a driving factor, but an obsessive compulsion, then you need to see what led to that. Then perhaps you will understand, not necessarily agree, but understand what drove me to want to live what I thought I could finally achieve only as an adult, a normal life; for once, I would be just like everybody else.

Today I am older and wiser and I know that there is not a single definition of "normal," not for a person, not for a family. Everything is relative. When I ran the pharmaceutical company, we had an employee named Mary, and she had one limb, a leg. Babies are "normally" born with four limbs, two arms and hands, two legs and feet, and ten fingers and toes. And while Mary's physical condition was not statistically normal, it was normal for Mary. That's how she was made.

But that wisdom came with age, and when I was growing up, I didn't know that. I truly thought there was a standard of "normal" and although I didn't know quite what it was, I knew it wasn't us. I knew that we weren't a normal family. I knew that it wasn't the way it was supposed to be and knowing the difference made it worse. I could see normal and healthy but only if I pressed my nose up to the window—that door was never open. But inside that world,

I could see that people were calm and happy and safe. And I longed for it, my desire to leave my world and walk into theirs was strong but always out of my reach. I knew that someday I'd get out, someday I could make my own life and when I did, it would be normal.

Prologue

I was six when I saw my mother's first suicide attempt. It was horrifying and the affect it had on me was irreversible. But that event, in and of *itself*, didn't change me that much, I was already damaged. This was just the next act in the surreal farce that was my life as a child. Actually, it was almost oddly fitting, kind of like, so how you going to top that last one?

"Ladies and gentlemen, for my next trick I'm going to slash my wrists and bleed to death in front of my six-year-old son, you won't want to miss this."

Already by six my life was bizarre, and I knew it. They say that when something is all you've ever known, then it is your reality and, therefore, normal to you. This was never true for me, I knew there was something wrong with us, I knew we were not a normal family. I knew we were fucked up.

CHAPTER 1

Coward

It was the next day and we began the way we had countless mornings before. I would make her coffee while she slowly emerged from the inevitable hangover fog that engulfed her. Assuming we had been together, as we had on the previous evening, I would fill her in on the details for which she had zero recall. Sometimes it was funny, sometimes not. This particular evening had not been amusing.

I was ten years old and a burden to both of my parents. For my mom, who was not capable of taking care of herself, let alone children, I was an especially heavy load as I lived with her and only visited my father. You may think that it would be difficult for a ten-year-old boy to live without an adult taking care of him but I was accustomed to it. I took on the parental role because after they divorced, somebody had to.

The prior evening she had taken me along to go over to her friend's house for an evening of heavy drinking. All of her "friends" were drunks but they accepted that she had to bring me along. No one gave a second thought about getting staggering, falling down drunk in front of this little kid, and although it didn't faze me, I knew this was not the way it was supposed to be.

It was a school night (and work night) and we were at Don and Trudy's; the drinking had started early. I ate chips and dip for dinner that night. On the record player one song played over and over:

Bottle of wine
True to the vine
When you going to let me get sober
Leave me alone
Let me go home
Let me go home and start over

I sat by myself watching them drink and slowly transform into the ugly drunks that I knew all too well. It was kind of surreal, me sitting and always observing, and although there were any number of things I would rather have been doing, I didn't mind, because I had to watch over my mom. When I was with her, I could make sure she was safe and usually control her drinking somewhat. I wondered what the other kids in fourth grade were doing that night, probably homework, or having a family dinner, or playing with their friends. But I was on mom-duty, with a bunch of tragically drunk adults. I never talked about these nights with anyone and if asked, I made up ordinary things we had done together like going out to the movies.

Late in the evening, Trudy took a sudden interest in me and she came to the table and sat across from me babbling incoherently. I simply nodded my head and reached for more chips feigning interest as best I could. Eventually, I excused myself to use the bathroom and when I returned she was passed out on the floor in front of the stereo. Out cold, thankfully.

It was past 11 P.M., but I had never had bedtime so this was not unusual. After several failed attempts to awaken the drunken Trudester, Lora decided it was time to go and she staggered out to our car. I was used to her driving drunk but she was especially bad and so I delicately suggested we call a cab. Despite my care in suggesting this alternative, she snapped and flew into a rage, the precise behavior I was trying to avoid. Lora was a mean drunk and once she hit the tipping point she became abusive.

"Get in the Goddamned car, you little asshole, or I throw you in."

Thinking I had no choice and wanting to avoid driving her into deeper rage, I got in praying we would get pulled over by a cop. We took off and by the time we hit Highway 55, she was weaving across lanes while driving over the speed limit. I was terrified and I honestly thought I was going to die. I reached for the door handle and told her, "If you don't pull over, I swear to God I am going to jump out of this car, I mean it, Mom. Pull over, right now."

She ignored me. The fear and terror of this car ride gurgled up from my gut and I thought I was going to throw up. As my anxiety grew steadily I knew I had to do something so I opened the car door and told her again that I was going to jump. I wasn't just doing this to get her attention; I honestly thought I would have a better chance of surviving if I jumped out of a moving car. I sat looking down at the pavement of the highway as it sped by underneath us, calculating how to do it. It's hard when you are ten years old and those are your only two choices; stay in the car and get killed or jump out of the car and hope you survive.

Of course, I wasn't wearing a seatbelt and as I sat on the edge of the car seat holding the car door open she looked over at me not saying a word. We sat there frozen in time, a stand-off, and for a brief second I thought she would come to her senses. I was wrong. She turned and looked straight ahead and pushed the gas pedal all the way down to the floor. I could see the speedometer rapidly moving up; we were approaching 90 miles an hour when I finally shut the door.

Only then did she let up on the gas. I couldn't stop shaking. I looked over at her and she was smiling, a victory smile; she had won. This had been a game to her. She drove on never looking at me. All she said to me was "Coward."

That was the last and only thing she said to me for the rest of the night. By the grace of God we made it home to our slum apartment and when she managed to park the car she simply got out and walked to our place never looking back. I sat in the car, hating my life, hating her, and hating everyone for being trapped in this hellhole. Where was my father, what was he doing tonight, or my brothers, where were they or anyone of my friends, I was sure they were all safe in bed. I wanted to run away. But of course, I couldn't, the only way I was ever going to get out was if I could survive and grow up. Then I could leave, just as the others had. I felt sad and ashamed and I was no longer scared. I didn't care what happened.

Other than Lora, I never told anyone about it. And even as I write this I can't believe how horrible it must have been, but for me at the time, it was just another bad night.

In the light of day, she was sincerely mortified that she had endangered me and she wept and held me very tight. She said she was sorry, she said she was a horrible mother, she said she loved me more than anything in the world.

And I cried too, because I knew all of it was true and I could never get out.

Chapter 2

In the Beginning

George and Lora were very remarkable people. They met in 1947 in El Centro, California. George was tall, handsome, and charming. He was the first son of Greek immigrant parents, a born alpha-child. He was a ladies' man and he happened to be an outstanding athlete. After the war he was living his dream—drafted by the Cleveland Indians, he moved to California, where the team played off season, he moved to play ball in the minor league hoping for his big break.

Lora was just nineteen when she met George. They were both at a social dance listening to a big band. Lora had come with a date and spotted George standing across the room talking with friends. She would later say that she thought he was the most handsome man she had ever seen. She insisted that her date take her over and make an introduction. With his dark complexion, piercing brown eyes, and black wavy hair, she decided this gorgeous man in the double-breasted suit was either a movie star or a gangster, and either way she was determined to have him.

Even by nineteen, Lora was used to getting what she wanted. She was beautiful with high cheekbones, wavy auburn hair, and soft gray eyes. She was on the tall side for women of that time, five foot seven, and weighed 98 pounds. She was intelligent and witty and sought after by virtually every single man in town. By both accounts, their meeting was like a chemical reaction (similar to a minor explosion) and they fell deeply and passionately in love at once.

Lora got George a job in town so he could work and earn extra money when he wasn't playing ball. One day he complained about having to room with all the guys so while he was at work, she drove his car over to the boarding house, packed up his things, and moved him into her father's home where he shared a bed with my grandfather. Years later, he would laugh about that particular incident and talk about just how typical that was of her; she just took charge, didn't ask permission, and if she wanted something and was determined to get it, she usually did.

These early days together were high energy, high laughter, and high passion. Lora didn't drink, she was popular and knew virtually everyone in town, and she was adventurous and fun. George was an "all out kind of man"; worked hard, played hard, drank and smoked, and truly lived life to the fullest. They made a beautiful couple and both of them would recall that time in their lives as happy and exciting. But George was getting restless. It was the off-season and he needed to find work. He was also feeling too controlled. Everything he had, outside of baseball, was Lora's. He thought their relationship was changing; it was going from fun and carefree to serious albeit romantic. She was just a kid to him, still a teenager. Better to stop things now before it became complicated. He'd been through this many times with many women but this time it would be different. He would miss her; he knew that. There was something about her that was different than the others. The next day after Lora went to work, without saying a word to her, he packed up all his things in his car and he left her.

Lora came home that night after work not only to discover that he was gone, but that he had abandoned her without leaving a note or saying goodbye. She was alone. The next morning she called in sick to work and went to the train station and bought a ticket to go to a town six hours away in Northern California. She knew she had to find him. She was in love with him and she knew she wanted to spend the rest of her life with him so she wasn't about to just let him slip away. She recalled that on the very first night they met he mentioned in passing that he had a buddy from Detroit that he grew up with who had moved to California. She didn't know his friend's name but she did remember the name of the town. That's all she had to go by; it was a long shot, he could be anywhere, but she was determined to find him, so she would start there.

George's visit was a complete surprise to his friend Tony, although a pleasant one. They were childhood friends who grew up together and hadn't seen each other for years. George told Tony that he had come to California to play ball and in the off-season he was looking for a job. He asked if he could stay, but unfortunately Tony's in-laws were staying at the house for a week so there was no room. George asked if it would be okay for him to sleep in his car parked in his driveway. He planned to get up the next morning and start applying for jobs. George slept in his car and when he woke up he drove into town to a gas station. While the attendant filled the gas tank and serviced the car, he went inside to the men's room to freshen up and shave.

When the train arrived Lora got out to find a taxi station. She didn't know the town or even where to begin looking for him, so when she got in the cab and the driver asked, "Where to?" She told him honestly, "I don't know, just start driving." The driver asked if she would like to head into town and that seemed to make sense to her—it was as good a place as any to begin her search. They drove up and down the streets and as time went on she began to feel more and more pessimistic and foolish. What on earth was she thinking? How could she possibly ride around a strange town, which she had no idea if he would go to, and simply expect to run into him? The whole thing seemed ridiculous as she rode around and around. After a long time, they came to an intersection at a stoplight and the driver asked, "Miss, do you want me to take you back to the train station now?" "Yes," she said, "but go around the block one more time."

George finished shaving, combed his hair, straightened his tie and got into his car. He put the key into the ignition, started the car and heard a familiar voice from the back seat say, "Hello, George." He looked in the mirror and recognized at once the gray eyes looking back at him.

She had spotted his car as it drove through the intersection while she was stopped at the light. She simply told the driver, "Follow that car." When he went into the men's room she got out and climbed into the back seat and ducked down until he put his key in the ignition. She knew she had to have him. He knew she would get what she wanted. What she didn't know, and he didn't know, is that she was pregnant. And that is how our family started.

CHAPTER 3

Growing Up Phill

FIRST, LET'S DEFINE CHILDHOOD. My childhood wasn't anything like your's. In fact, it wasn't like anyone's that I know. It just shouldn't have been that bad, I knew that even as a kid. After all, we were a white, upper-middle-class family. We lived in a nice home in an affluent neighborhood. My father was an executive and my mother stayed at home. They were a beautiful and popular couple, known for their hospitality and fabulous parties. We had advantages that most people never get, so even as a kid I wondered how we could be so fucked up.

Despite the fact that George and Lora were a beautiful and popular couple, the problems underneath were horrifying. She was a woman with mental illness and an addiction to alcohol. And though gregarious and generous to the outside world, he was selfish and dominant and tended only to his needs. Both of them were unpredictable and unreliable. If they wanted to go out and get drunk, they did, it didn't matter that they were supposed to be at my school choir concert or pick me up to take me to a school dance. She did it because of her addiction, he did it because he only did what he wanted to. What made it worse was the inconsistency. If they felt like it, they could act like real parents; I just never knew when that would be. And so from an early age, I began to worry. All children need stability and to know there is someone upon whom they can rely; not having that would create a lasting void for which I spent most of my adult years trying to compensate.

Today, addiction and mental illness are openly talked about, and it is nothing for which a person should feel ashamed. *People* magazine routinely tells us the celebrities who are in rehab and commercials advertise psychotropic drugs for treatment of a wide range of mental or psychological disorders. This was not the case when I was growing up, there was no Betty Ford clinic, no commercials about the benefits of antidepressant. It wasn't talked about. My mother was someone who needed help, intervention on many levels, but instead she was blamed for her erratic behavior. Her own mother had been taken away and institutionalized when Lora was just four years old.

The terrors of our home life were easily disguised to the outside world. After all, she was intelligent, witty, engaging, and capable of parenting on some levels. One minute functional, the next out of control. Early on there were signs and incidences that were alarming. My father ignored them. He was too proud to have a mentally disturbed wife and the truth is he was also too selfish. The only time my father ever acknowledged her problems is when he left her and they were divorcing, and then it was only to make her look bad to anyone who would listen.

"Growing up in our household was incredibly difficult and painful. It shaped who I became and the choices I made."

CHAPTER 4

Tools for Survival

SO, I HAVE THIS INCREDIBLE MEMORY; I mean really, I can recall my first nightmare when I was just in diapers. I dreamt my brothers came in and took me out of my crib and left me in the living room, and in my dream I was frightened because all the doors were closed and I couldn't reach the door knobs. By three, I could recite "The Lord's Prayer" from beginning to end, without prompting. My mother said it astounded people. They were just words, I didn't understand what they meant but I could memorize them. That is how far back my memory goes and the extent to which I can remember the smallest details. And even as a young child, I remember always feeling angst-ridden. I wasn't born that way; it was a natural reaction to my environment.

Everything was always unpredictable. Perhaps the only consistent thing in my life growing up was inconsistency. I never knew who would show up. Sometimes, they were attentive and parental. For example, of the few principles they shared, hospitality and good manners were essential. We were raised to be courteous and polite. At the same time, they were thoughtless and neglectful parents, self-absorbed drunks. They may not remember your birthday, or they could show up drunk (or not at all) to your fourth-grade choir concert, but God forbid you should forget to say *please* and *thank you* or neglect covering your mouth when you coughed. It was weird, but typical of the juxtaposition of people and circumstances that made up my life. Beautiful, well-to-do, popular parents, raising children in a little shop of horrors.

By the time I turned five, I was terrified of the nighttime; not the night itself, or the dark, or any of that, but when the day was over, it meant it was time to go to bed. The nights were the worst part of my life. That's when my brothers fell asleep, and that's when their fighting and screaming always woke me up. When my own kids went to bed at night we tucked you in, I said prayers with you and read you stories. With Itsie, until you were twelve, I even stayed in your room until you fell asleep. It was routine, something your mother and I never had to think about, we just did it and wanted to do it, part of the privileges of parenthood. I never knew that sort of life, not once. We were told to go to sleep and I would lie awake dreading what could happen next.

Once they started, I usually put my head under the covers and wished with all my might that it would stop. Sometimes I would open the door and sneak down the hallway to see what they were fighting about. I would lie there in darkness on the floor at the end of the hallway. Sometimes I did this for hours. From there I had a perfect view of the rest of the house and no one could see me. On one particularly bad evening they were yelling and swearing at each other and I went down the hall just in time to see my father hit my mother and knock her to the floor. She laid there not moving. My dad just stood there standing over her and looking down. After a while when she didn't get back up, he went across the street to Dr. Warren's house and Dr. and Mrs. Warren came back to check on my mom. Mrs. Warren got a towel with some ice and Dr. Warren applied it to her head and was looking her over while Mrs. Warren held her hand. My mother told them she tripped and hit her head on the counter.

I sat in the hallway in the darkness. They didn't know I was there, but I had seen the whole thing. I knew she was lying and it confused me. Then I got it. She wanted to keep it a secret because it was wrong. This is not what is supposed to happen in families and so she made up a story so no one would know the truth; this also left an indelible impression. I was beginning to see how the world worked and the tools you needed to survive.

I don't know what occupies the mind of a typical five- or six-year-old because I was never a typical child. By that age, I was figuring out survival rules. I was learning and practicing how to keep secrets, make up stories, and act "as if." I just pretended to be a kid; I never was one.

So, from an early age I learned how to not let anyone in, to pretend that everything was okay, and to suppress thoughts and feelings, especially if they were sad or frightening. By the time I met my wife, I was an expert, no one really knew who I was, not even my closest friends. As an adult, I was an accomplished actor, careful not to disclose my identity or how I really felt. If I had doubts about my sexuality or my parenting abilities, they were all suppressed immediately and locked away.

I believe that children are capable of processing new information much more rapidly than their adult counterparts. What they experience does not need to be filtered through years of conditioning, previous knowledge, or cognitive bias.

What I saw that night had an immediate impact on me, and in turn, I processed the events and they were imprinted, forever in my mind. Not just what I saw but *what it told me about my parents*, *about adults*, and *about the world.* The yelling and arguing was not just a lot of harmless noise.

"Quit worrying," my brothers would tell me.

"I can't help it, it scares me."

"It's just like thunder, it's scary when it's loud but it isn't dangerous, thunder can't hurt you."

But lightning can kill you. And sometimes when there is thunder, there is lightning, you just never know when. Therefore, I knew that their arguing, like thunder, should be taken seriously as a warning of what could come; a severe deadly storm.

Chapter 5

Mother

LORA WAS THE YOUNGEST OF SEVEN CHILDREN. She was a "change of life" baby born twenty years after some of her older siblings. Her mother was taken away to a mental ward when she was four. She remembered constantly asking to see her mother for eight years but she was never allowed. Her years growing up were filled with neglect and almost constant abandonment. She was cast from one family member to the next. She would later recall having to wait in the kitchen while her older siblings argued over who had to take her next.

"Well, hell, we've had her for six months. It's someone else's turn."

Wherever she landed it was understood she was there to work. There were children to watch or chores to do; she had to earn her keep. This was hard on her but not as bad as the times when no one would take her, that meant she had to go back with her dad.

He was a simple man, but tired and ill equipped to take care of a child; he had never had that role with any of his other children. She remembered him taking her up to the pool hall and telling her to sit on the curb and wait. Hours would go by and eventually he would stagger out drunk and she would lead him home.

When she married George, she longed for stability, and to be wanted. Their early lives together were much less marred by the problems that would eventually tear them apart. Their extended family all lived close by. There are wonderful home movies that capture these times. My father's siblings getting married, more babies including my brother Peter four years after Nick. But there were signs of trouble as well. George had a hard time settling into a "quiet life." He would drink hard, gamble, stay out all night, and Lora was turning more and more to alcohol. Everyone recalls them as a beautiful couple, witty and intelligent, excellent hosts for wonderful parties. But they also recall the volatile nature of their romance; passionate one moment and fiercely at each other's throats the next.

He worked, she stayed home. They were the ones that the younger siblings turned to when they needed help or advice. He was the kind of father that most men were of that generation. He didn't change diapers or do other chores he considered "women's work." Both of my Greek aunts had similar arrangements with their husbands but they had been raised to expect this; that was simply how marriage worked and they accepted it.

Lora was not raised to be anyone's wife. In fact, she was never really raised by anyone in the sense that her own mother was taken away to an asylum and her father didn't have the skill or interest in raising a small child. So she mostly raised herself. She was intelligent and she learned how to survive and therefore was used to being very independent. She did not accept that the man was the head of the household. She was a loving mother but not an attentive one. Someone else in the family usually wiped a nose or washed the faces of her boys.

Lora hated housework and did not derive any pleasure in childcare. She loved her boys but she would have been very content going off to work and having someone else look after them. George was a dominant firstborn Greek male raised from birth to believe that women were to be taken care of and that, in turn, his job was to have the responsibility of head of the house. This philosophical difference between them proved to be a greater challenge to their long-term commitment and was the root cause of many of their growing number of arguments.

Lora had started drinking initially because George got to. She quickly grew tired of sitting in the kitchen with the ladies while the men played cards and got drunk. Soon she was drinking with them and she would join them in whatever activities the guys were up to. Most of the guys didn't mind and even George thought it was cute when his young bride would get a little tipsy. But in later years, after she finally quit drinking, she told me that she was an alcoholic before she ever took her first drink. She believed she was born that way. And so it got progressively worse over the years. But at first, in the beginning, she could more or less control it.

George was brought up with a clear understanding of the differences in the roles of a man and a woman. He did not understand why his own wife, who was far better off than the other women in his family, did not appreciate her life and all that he did to make it possible. His sisters were appreciative and grateful for their husbands. They wanted to stay home, raise their children and clean and cook for their husbands.

This was simply not Lora. She tried it all and everything she attempted she did exceedingly well. She learned to cook, sew, bake and truly excelled at everything. But she was bored with all of it. She, in turn, did not understand or accept that her husband wanted her to be just another housewife. They began to resent each other more and more. Each began to rebel, to drink, and to argue endlessly.

Despite the problems, he continued to do well in his career. But times were changing for the family and extended family. George's parents were moving to Florida following his father's retirement. Within a year, the rest of his siblings and their families would follow. That meant George and Lora were alone in Detroit. The network of family and the safety net they provided were gone. He was promoted and would travel for the next three years most of the time.

Lora was alone with her two boys and pregnant.

By the time I was born, her drinking and depression had progressed to an alarming degree. She became wildly unpredictable, loving and kind one moment and angry and abusive the next. She would stay up late at night drinking, and sometimes on these occasions she would wake up one of her boys. One night when George was on the road, after a heavy night of drinking, she went in and woke up her oldest boy. She dragged Nick into the kitchen and took a serrated knife and held it to her throat and asked him, "Do you want to see me cut my throat, do you?"

I wonder was he scared, did he measure every breath, every word, not knowing what would happen next? Or was he so tired of this drama that he felt secretly guilty for wishing she would follow through for once and let everyone live their lives in peace? Either reaction would be understandable. This was the family and the environment where I spent the first four years of my life.

Chapter 6

The Final Years

IT APPARENTLY WASN'T ALWAYS THAT WAY. Relatives, and even my brothers, talk about times when my mother didn't drink and my father came home at least sometimes. My mother would take a bus to get my brothers to church on Sundays. Our family, and our extended family of Greek relatives, all lived in and around the Detroit area and there are many stories about how close they all were and how they were there for each other. This is not the family I knew and those two people were not my parents. When I was four, we moved to Minnesota after the rest of our family all moved to Florida. We were alone and isolated. My mother's depression and alcoholism got progressively worse and my father's response to this was to drink and stay away.

The fighting, the arguments, the drinking, all became part of a real-life soap opera for the neighborhood. I learned to cover up what really happened so no one would know the truth about how bad it was. I learned from them, I watched it the night he hit her and knocked her out.

"We heard your mom did it on purpose."

"Yeah, did she?"

"No, I told you it was an accident."

"My mom said she had to go to a mental institute."

"Did she weave you any baskets?"

General laughter.

"She went to California because my uncle died. And if you believe that, then you probably think she's the Easter Bunny and wove your Easter basket."

Even louder laughter.

I would laugh with them but I wanted to cry, the pain and the hurt was real. Sometimes I think it would have been easier if they were two horrible and wretched people, then I guess that you would just expect them to do horrible and wretched things. But they weren't, and as a child it made me angry that they didn't try harder or figure it out. They were gifted with beauty and brains and talent and they could have done so much for themselves and their children. It's weird, but despite all of their problems, I was proud of them and proud to be their son. And despite the abuse to each other and to us, we were raised to be polite and courteous, to be good and decent people. And I knew they loved us; there were too many times I felt neglected and abused but never unloved, if that makes any sense.

So, let me share with you an example of their parenting styles, it happened the first time I apparently said "fuck." We had just moved to Minnesota and one Saturday my parents decided to paint the bedroom my brother Peter and I shared. I was terribly excited about it, I loved it when anytime, for any reason, we did things all together, like a real family. So like any hyper five-year-old, I kept asking my dad, "When can I help?" I was the only one without a job and my dad kept putting me off, saying, "Not yet, wait 'til we're done with this part." Well, every new thing they did became "this part" and when almost every wall was painted and they were finishing the last coat on the last wall I pleaded, "Dad, you said I could help, can't I paint now?" And he got pissed and shouted, "No, painting is not for five-year-olds." I felt completely dejected, lied to, and it seemed unbearably unfair to me so I stuffed my hands in my pocket and, it just came out.

"Oh, fuck."

Everything stopped. My father lowered his rolling brush. My brothers looked at each other trying not to laugh and my mother turned from the wall and carefully eyed my father waiting to see what would happen next. I knew in that instant that I had said or done something really bad, but the truth is whatever I said, I said by accident. My father stood eyeing me.

"What did you just say?"

"I don't know."

"Where did you hear that? Who taught you that word?"

Immediate suspicion was cast upon my two brothers and my father spun around and turned on them yielding his paint roller like a saber.

"Which one of you taught him this?"

Both brothers defaulted to instant pleas of innocence swearing on their lives it had not been them.

"Well, he couldn't have just made it up, I'll deal with you two later."

With this he turned his attention to me and to this day I remember the verbal beating I took as a result of saying something I could not recall and whose meaning I did not know. In my whole life, my father never hit me but he could verbally and emotionally brutalize anyone. He could bring grown men to tears and had on many occasions. The fact that I was only five made no difference to him, there was no George Lite.

By the time I left the room I did not feel like I was worth anything, I felt I was a stupid and hideous child, ungrateful and disrespectful. Even my brothers, who usually delighted in seeing me get into trouble, looked like they felt bad for me. I just turned and walked out tears brimming in my eyes but refusing to cry in front of all of them. He had succeeded in making me feel like I was a terrible child, stupid and worthless. The tears poured down my face when I got out of the room and I walked to the basement stairs to sit alone.

Now, okay, as a parent I get that you have some choices to make in these situations with your small child. But, really? Verbally abuse and berate your small child? And in front of everyone? First of all, who cares? Would it have really been so bad to say, "Here you go, little guy, take the brush and knock yourself out." That's what your mother and I would have done. "Great job! Now go wash up." Then paint over. Second, sometimes children say things they either don't mean or don't understand. My own inclination in those situations with you kids was to ignore it and try not to laugh; however, I can understand the choice to make it a life lesson for your little one, but seriously, humiliating a five-year-old?

Here again, my mother had a choice she needed to make as to what to do next. She couldn't undo the damage that he had done, but how she chose to deal with it tells you about the kind of person she was. She wanted to attend to my needs and still show support to her husband and my father; tough job under the circumstances. I sat alone on the third step from the top, facing the wall and leaning my head against it. The door opened and my mom came in and sat on the step next to me. For what seemed like a long time we didn't talk, we both just sat in silence.

"How are you doing?"

"I'm alright."

"Boy, you took that well, I think I'd be a mess right now."

"I don't even know what I said."

"Well, it was a pretty bad word."

"What does it mean?"

"It means all kinds of horrible things and it scared your father."

"It scared him? He didn't act scared, he acted mean."

"Oh, my, yes, he always overreacts like that when he's frightened. He wants to protect you."

"Then why did he scream at me?"

"He doesn't know any other way. He thinks he needs to make an impression so that he can be sure you don't do that again. Believe it or not, he's trying to help you."

"Yeah, well, that didn't help, it just made me feel bad."

"Don't feel bad, it was a mistake."

"Then why did he say all those things?"

"Come here, you're crying."

"No, I'm not."

"Yes, you are, let me hold you. You are an amazing young man and I am very proud of you. And your father is too. He just likes to carry on and make a lot of noise, kind of like an animal in the jungle."

"Like a monkey?"

"More like a baboon."

It cheered me up.

Chapter 7

Tall Tales and the Cowardly Lion

The fundamental duty that every parent has to their child is to grow up feeling safe and protected; Lora and George didn't quite get that. They loved their kids but that whole concept of prioritizing the children's needs above their own was foreign to them. I never felt safe or protected.

I guess it was the unpredictability that made me feel unsafe, and even as a kid, I knew those two couldn't protect me, they could hardly take care of themselves. It was as though after all these years they still hadn't figured out what children need and how to take care of them.

Halloween is a really big deal for a child. I remember Halloween the year I started kindergarten. All the kids in the neighborhood talked about it for weeks and weeks. Like all kids that age, we were obsessed. All the houses in the neighborhood were decorated with the usual creepy Halloween gore, except ours. Everyone had their costume, except me. By the way, this is how I learned about what was "normal"—from other children and other families. I knew that by now my parents should have taken me to get a costume and bought some decorations and of course candy for the trick-or-treaters. But they hadn't and as it got closer and closer to Halloween I began to get more and more anxious rather than excited like the other kids. But here's the trick, I never let on. I acted as though it didn't bother me or worry me in the least. I had no one to talk to, no one in whom I could confide. And this ability to pretend, to deny the reality, and talk with no one and keep it all to myself are the tools that got me through growing up and also living most of my adult life as a straight male.

I would sit on the bus and listen to my friends talk excitedly about their costumes and actively participate as though everything was fine. All the kids were excited and anticipating a wonderful time, so I acted like I was too. But five-year-old Phillip was fooling everyone. He wasn't excited, he was worried. And because my parents were unpredictable, I wasn't sure how the story would end. Deep down, I figured they would never let me down on such an important event, but you never knew with them. They promised they would get everything. I made them promise. I thought they would come through.

So then it was Halloween. On the way home from school we talked about how we would eat dinner as quickly as we could and gather together and start trick-or-treating. When I got off the bus I ran home and tore into the house anxious to see the costume they got for me. Only there was no costume, there were no decorations, and of course we didn't have candy to pass out. My mother didn't drive, so there was no way to get my costume and the candy until my father came home from work. Usually he didn't come right home after work, he stopped at the bars. Sometimes he didn't come home until late at night. But even so, I was still sure he would come home early, probably he was getting everything right now while we're waiting, I told my mom, "I'll sit right here," I told her, on the bench by the window so I could see him when he drove up. I still feel bad for the little boy who spent all afternoon sitting on the bench by the window waiting and hoping that his father would come home so that he could go out trick-or-treating.

My mom tried to help; she offered to cut some holes in a sheet or to make a mask out of a paper bag. "Let's just make our own costume," she said, but I told her he would come. Besides, I knew all the kids would laugh at me, and they would know that I didn't have a costume; it would be obvious to everyone.

He never came. I sat on the bench looking out the window waiting for him to come home until the trick-or-treaters started to come out. Then we turned all the lights out and sat in the den in the dark with only the glow of our television. I could hear the other kids trick-or-treating, I could hear them laughing and running around, occasionally they would knock on the door and call my name. I was heartbroken. Not even on Halloween? Not even this one day could we just be like a normal family? All I wanted was to go out trick-or-treating like all the other kids, was that so much? I sat in the dark in that den hating my life.

The next morning everybody was talking about how much fun they had and sharing stories and repeating funny things and of course everyone wanted to know where I was, and why I didn't join them. I told them we decided to go over to my cousins and I made up a story about this elaborate costume I had of the Cowardly Lion and that I got more candy and had more fun than I ever had before. I joined in on all the talk, the stories, and the laughter. I made up all this shit about where we went, details about the night, I even threw in a bunch of teenagers throwing eggs at a car and the driver getting out and chasing them. They believed every word. They never suspected a thing.

Chapter 8

Mom Ate a Raisin

IT WAS A WEEKEND, had to be because my dad was home, and I think it was summer because I know it was hot outside. My parents weren't speaking to each other, which meant we were in the danger zone. My brothers and I knew that as bad as it was when my parents were fighting and yelling at each other, it was much safer than when they weren't speaking. As a young child, the way in which I dealt with being sad, or depressed, or worried, was to seek out refuge in a place where I could be alone. I'm still like that to this day. On this particular day, I went outside and sat at the end of our driveway.

I was sitting throwing stones across the street wondering how this would play out and what I could do to keep them together. While I was pondering this, my brother Peter came running out of the front door of our house and went racing across the street to Dr. Warren's house, where he began frantically pounding on the screen door, calling over and over again, "DR. WARREN, YOU HAVE TO COME OVER, MOM ATE A RAISIN! DR. WARREN! PLEASE HURRY, MOM ATE A RAISIN!"

Just after he burst through the front door I looked over and saw my older brother Nick, he had the complete opposite demeanor, he walked out slowly and stood on the front step. Where Peter was panicked and screaming, Nick was calm, not moving, and on his face you could see profound sadness as though the weight of the world was resting on his adolescent shoulders, a look in his eyes that he would carry with him for the rest of his life.

In his panic, Peter broke open the screen door and ran into the house. I didn't understand the situation at all. I was confused by the contrast in my two brothers' behavior and it didn't make any sense to me that Peter would be panicked over Mom eating a raisin or that she would need a doctor. However, Dr. Warren came running out of his front door with my brother carrying his black doctor bag and the three of them went inside the house.

I got up and decided to go in and see for myself what all the fuss was about. When I entered the house, I knew that something was terribly wrong. They were all screaming at each other.

"Grab her arms!"

"No, careful, get it out of her hand!"

"Watch out."

"Lora, we're trying to help you!"

I ran down the hall to my parents' bedroom, and with all the chaos, no one noticed me standing in the doorway.

The first thing I remember was the blood; it was everywhere. I had never seen so much blood, it was all over my mom and the guys, on the furniture, and there were pools of blood on the floor. In fact, they were having a hard time restraining her because they kept slipping on the blood on the floor. My mom was at the center, she was fighting them and making these really strange, scary guttural noises, like an animal. She didn't talk, just sort of barked out sounds. The guys were all bigger and stronger but they couldn't hold her and they were having trouble getting her to settle down and cooperate. I ran into the room and went right up to her and my dad immediately shouted for someone to "get him out of here." But there was no one available to get me out so I ran right up to her and I started yelling, "Mom, Mom, are you okay? Mom, we're trying to help you, you're hurt."

What happened next put the final nail in the coffin of my so-called childhood. It still haunts me to this day. At that time in my life, it was the most frightening thing that ever happened to me.

She didn't recognize me.

I was six years old and my own mother didn't know who I was.

And in that moment I knew that I was all alone. Phillip had no one in this world he could really count on, no one to protect him or take care of him. It is why later I accepted God so readily into my life. I will never forget; it was much worse than the blood and chaos. For me, it was a "the call is coming from inside the house" moment. That precise second in time when you realize *Oh, fuck, this is bad, this is really bad.* The impression and the lesson learned about life was immediate. Fifty years later, I can see her face and the vacant look in her steel-grey eyes, but mostly, I can feel the terror as though I was there again; she doesn't know me.

After that, no one had to drag me out of the room, I went outside on my own to be alone. I watched them take her away to the hospital with my dad driving Dr. Warren's car and Dr. Warren holding the towel around her wrists trying to hold her down in the back seat. I realized what my brother Peter was really saying:

"Mom cut herself with the razor."

She was away for a long time and my brothers stayed with my dad and I went and stayed with Mrs. Magnusson and her family. Not too long after she came back, my dad moved out. That's when things got really bad.

CHAPTER 9

The Facts about the Birds and Bees

MY FATHER MOVED OUT and my oldest brother went away to college and I thought they were the lucky ones. It seemed to me they had escaped. There would be an intense divorce battle between my parents; this was prior to the "irreconcilable differences" divorces we know of today. She would sue him for mental cruelty and he countersued accusing her of being an unfit mother. Battle lines were drawn and friends, family, even vague acquaintances were forced to choose sides and testify in court. This would drag on for five years.

Strangely, they actually continued to see each other after he moved out for a while and so of course I was convinced they would get back together. He would come back home for dinner on Sunday and we would go over to his new apartment and my mom and I would spend the weekend.

My father had moved into an apartment complex with an eclectic group of middle-aged swingers. Keep in mind this was the late 60s. Men in their forties wore bellbottoms and sported long Elvis sideburns, and middle-aged women wore miniskirts and everyone tried to be hip. Even middle-aged adults were not immune to the sexual revolution and the free spirit of the decade. Most of his new friends were single, and everyone drank and partied excessively. This is where I met "Cookie," the divorcee who made the rounds sleeping with every new available man. Jack and Barb, the first unmarried couple I had ever met that lived together, and John, the wealthy restaurant owner who was a raging alcoholic. Not long after he moved in, my mother found out that when she wasn't there spending time with my father he had begun dating a pretty, young, single blonde named Barbara. That last weekend they spent together she confronted him. They were both drinking and he denied the whole thing. My mother took me home that Sunday afternoon and continued to drink and smoke and seethe. Then she got up, grabbed me by the hand, and said we were going over to meet the other woman. I pleaded with her not to do that, I reminded her that my father said nothing was going on between them but she wanted to see her face to face and to confront her. It was important to her that her eight-year-old son witness all of this. We drove over to his apartment complex and she marched me down the hall and when she got to the apartment she banged on the door. Fortunately, no one answered and I was terribly relieved. As we left the building and headed to the parking lot my mother happened to look over to the second-floor screened-in porch that belonged to my father's apartment and saw my dad and the young blonde making out on the lawn chair. She grabbed me by the hand and took me up to a place where I could see clearly.

"Look, look right up there, you see?"

"I don't see anything."

"Right there on your father's patio, he's there with that blonde whore, making love."

I didn't want to look, I didn't want to see anything because if it were true, it meant they were never going to get back together and I had tried so hard and hoped so much. I didn't want it all to fall apart. But it was clear that we weren't leaving until she proved it to me. So I lied.

"Yes, I see it, can we go home now?"

On the ride home in the car I just sat there, very quiet, wanting to cry. Any hopes that I had for getting the two of them back together were gone.

From that point on, it was a balls-out, take-no-prisoners, scorched-earth battle. When my father left, my mother was forced to go back to work—the first job she took was at a local hotel called the Ambassador. We were still in the house then, and it was probably one of the few places she could start working at because it was close. She didn't have a driver's license, she had not driven a car for years, and she had no formal education or training. While she was married to my father, she was the boss's wife, a stay-at-home mom, and an excellent cook and hostess. But culinary skills and being a wonderful conversationalist didn't qualify her to find work and we needed the money. So she took a job as a coat check lady and took a cab to and from work because it was only a two-dollar fare. She continued drinking a lot and both of them dedicated as much time and effort as they could to convince their children to hate the other parent. It became their quest.

My father would spend hours talking about my mother and, at least when they were with him, my brothers would actively participate in these conversations. I would get very upset and oftentimes I would start crying. This is when my father would turn to my brothers and say, "There she is, boys, let's get little Phillip a dress and maybe some ribbons for his hair, look at him crying just like a little girl."

He really seemed to enjoy taunting me because he would say it over and over and get right in my face, "Is that what you are, is that what you are, Philip, just a little girl? You sure cry like one."

One afternoon, my dad started in yet again about my mother. Today's topic was "Why your mother is a whore." I was not a good pupil and he was getting agitated with me. He explained to me that the only reason she took a job at a hotel was so she could sleep with men. Finally, I just told him, "So what if she is, when I stayed with the Magnussons I slept with Lisa."

The light went on.

"You don't get it, do you?" He started laughing. "Let me tell you what happens when your mother sleeps with a man."

That's when my father sat me down and told me the facts about sex. First, he gave me an anatomy lesson, although I knew girls didn't have a penis, I did not know they had a vagina. It was essential that my father explain this in order to have the full impact of what I was about to learn. Then, using my mother and a never-ending stream of nameless, faceless men in a hotel room, George explained the facts of life to his eight-year-old son.

"Your mother takes off all her clothes and lies in the bed naked. Then the man takes off his clothes and his penis is hard. He lays on top of her and she has to spread her legs so he can get his hard penis inside her vagina."

I felt sick to my stomach. I wanted to throw up but I knew that would please him. I didn't move, I just stared at him showing no emotion. Afterward, as though suddenly hit with a spasm of parental responsibility, he added, "Now this is a very private discussion and you are not to share this with any of the other kids or friends."

The only good thing about that day is, in fact, it made me one of the most popular kids in all of third grade. I routinely held court, boys only, on the playground during lunch hour by the slide.

Chapter 10

Who's the Boss?

The years that followed after they finally split were full of drinking, fighting, a lot of drama, and neglect. I think in some way both of them felt liberated to not be tied down in a failing marriage, and I know they certainly enjoyed the freedom and excitement of dating and drinking. And it did have some perks for me, my father would hang out with the swingers at the apartment complex and on the weekends when he had me, he brought me to the parties. Most of the parties were held at Mr. N's place. I would be brought along on Friday and Saturday nights while all of the grown-ups got drunk and played cards and pool. Although it doesn't sound like much fun for a kid, I didn't mind. I got to be with my dad and I missed him when he wasn't there. I had little or no supervision at home or with my dad. We would come into the smoke-filled apartment and go to the room where the pool table was and I got to sit and play all night on the one-armed bandit that Mr. N had. There was always a never-ending supply of nickels. I was the only kid I knew who routinely got to stay up until one or two o'clock in the morning on weekends. And I also got to bartend—I learned how to make their drinks and empty their ashtrays so I didn't think it was all that bad.

The other advantage for me is that when each of my parents had me they never altered their lifestyle and so I got to go on a lot of dates, or at least I got to go out to dinner a lot. And my mom and dad went to the best restaurants in town. At a very young age I could order lobster tails, and I knew what kind of appetizers went best with the entrée.

I really wasn't supervised ever. I routinely failed to do any homework at all. My father never went to school conferences and my mother went sporadically so I rarely got into trouble. Never during those years did either one of my parents ever ask me if I had any homework. Never were there routines about this is what time we eat dinner, and this is when you do your homework, and this is what time you go to bed. No matter which parent I was with, they were almost always passed out before I went to bed.

My dad's relationship with Barb was getting more serious and I liked her very much. She had a very good influence on my father, and he began to pull out of his wild lifestyle. But at home, I was taking on more and more responsibility; I'm the only one who knew how to balance the checkbook; by the time I was eleven, I was writing out the checks for the bills and having my mom sign them. I knew how to do laundry, I knew how to talk to the bill collectors, and I knew how to call into work for her when she was too hung over to go in—I would tell her boss she had the flu.

So at a very early age I began to do what I could to take control of a life and an environment that seemed completely out of control to me. Abnormal became my normal. My mother would take me with her when she went over to drink with friends and I would find myself monitoring her alcohol intake.

"I think you've had enough, Mom, it's a workday tomorrow."

"Just one more, I promise, then we'll go."

"You said that two drinks ago."

This was about the time when her friends would chime in.

"I think your mother can decide when she wants to stop drinking, she is the adult."

To which I would usually shoot back something I only needed to say once.

"Really, she's not the one who will be calling in sick for her tomorrow if she's too hungover to work again, and if she calls in sick again she's going to get fired and by the way, we're three months behind on the rent and we've already gotten two eviction notices so, yeah, I don't think I'll be leaving this one up to her. Okay, Mom, one more and we need to go home."

Once we established who the adult was, they stayed out of it.

This was to be a pattern that was repeated over and over again when I was growing up. It wasn't always awful. We usually spent Saturday and Sunday mornings together with me going over what she did the night before. I would wait for her to get up and I would boil the water and make us each a cup of instant coffee. We would sit at the table and I would fill her in.

"And then, you and Lucille and Dee were all on your hands and knees and crawling on the floor around the coffee table."

"Oh my God, what in the hell were we doing that for?"

"You guys thought someone lost their contact."

"Who wears contacts?"

"No one. I told you that but at that point you guys were on a mission."

We both started laughing. It's weird, but it was my reality and I enjoyed those times together, at least when nothing really horrible happened.

As my dad began to settle down and live a fairly normal life, my mother continued to spiral out of control. Keep in mind, however, that they were still suing each other; the divorce had been going on for years. I knew I could never tell my father what was going on at home, because if I did, he would use it against my mother in court and take me away. I also knew that he didn't want to raise me, he wanted to hurt her. My brother Nick was gone. When he did come home from college he stayed with my father. My brother Peter was spending more and more time away, with his friends, getting heavily into drugs and alcohol. I had no one to turn to, no one that I could talk to about this.

Like all kids, I would fantasize to escape, but my fantasy wasn't about becoming a professional ballplayer or a rock star. My fantasy was that one day someone would come to the door in a uniform and take me away. I knew I could never leave, and I would never let anyone know what was really going on at home, but if the authorities came and took me away, then it wouldn't be my fault. In my fantasy, they would take me either to a boarding school or to a foster family. It didn't matter to me, either option was better than what I had. That fantasy got me through some very difficult times over the years.

Chapter 11

Love, Gratitude, and Forgiveness

THEN SOMETHING HAPPENED that would change my life forever. My Uncle Harry was visiting from Florida and my dad came and got me so we could all go out and eat. The real reason my dad wanted me along is so that Uncle Harry could drill me on what was going on at home and report back to my dad's family what a terrible mother Lora was. It was like an interrogation.

"So Phillip, tell me what you had for dinner last night?"

"What?"

"You know, dinner, what did you have last night?"

"Um, I don't remember."

"You don't remember or you didn't have dinner last night?"

"Well, yeah, like maybe last night I didn't have dinner, but Mom worked late."

"And she didn't leave dinner for you?"

"No, not last night."

"Well, how late did she work?"

"I don't know."

"But you just said she worked late last night."

"I know but she went out with friends after."

Uncle Harry looked over at my father.

"So how about lunch today, what did you have at school?"

"I didn't have lunch today, I didn't have lunch money."

After a few questions I stopped answering him. Normally I could think on my feet very quickly and make up answers—by ten I was really good at that. But for some reason, I let him peak inside before I shut the door.

My uncle turned to my father and said, "George, I have a great idea, I'll bring him with me down to Florida and have him spend the summer with Ma and Pa."

My heart just about jumped right out of my chest. This was the most exciting news I had ever heard. I loved my Greek yiayia and papau; in fact, I loved all my aunts and uncles and cousins. I immediately went into the ten-year-old "Dad, can I please, oh please, oh please" mode. My dad said he'd check with my mother and she said it was okay. It was the first thing I could recall them agreeing on in years. Now when I look back at it, it makes so much sense—neither one of them wanted the responsibility of care and feeding a young kid and to ship me off for the whole summer was a welcomed break for both of them.

Whatever the reason, that conversation, that decision, that moment in time forever changed my life. You may not believe me but I am convinced it was an act of God, I think he had had enough. The difference it would make in my life was immeasurable. Everything positive about how I dealt with the things in my life, how I survived, how I learned to forgive, came from that moment. I think the four years I was able to spend my entire summers with them saved my life.

My uncle cooked up this elaborate plan of how he would bring me down there and surprise everyone. My Aunt Tiner never married and lived with my grandparents. I flew back to Florida with my uncle and he drove me over to their house in Clearwater. I was to count to 100 and then come in the house. My uncle got up and went in to talk to Yiayia and Papau and Tiner. When I finished counting I got up and walked in the front door. I was kind of nervous because they hadn't actually seen me in a few years. When I walked in my aunt screamed, "Phillip!" and they were all over me. It was a big fat Greek welcome, with Yiayia and Tiner smothering me with kisses and hugs. I knew immediately that this was where I belonged.

It was nothing like my home, nothing. It was my sanctuary. It was the first time in my life I felt safe and protected, and taken care of. For the first time in my life it felt normal: There were routines, we ate three meals a day, we went to church on Sundays, and I was supervised and cared for. All children deserve this, but it was completely foreign to me. This was a new and wonderful experience. I felt secure and protected. I had a real family that loved me and cared for me. I had never been cared for, I was used to caring for someone else. I was "To Agori," Greek for "The Boy," and I was fawned over like a prince. Every summer after that it was the same, "When is The Boy coming?" And for the first time, I didn't have to pretend, there was nothing to hide. I didn't need to "act as if" we were a normal loving family because, in fact, we were.

They gave me my faith. The greatest gift I ever received from anyone came from my YiaYia and Papau that first summer. I was ten years old but older beyond my years. I had seen and experienced things most adults had not endured. Their faith was as deep and entrenched as the roots of giant tree in the forest. It was solid and had sustained them though all of the tremendous challenges they had faced in their lives. Whatever your views, it is an undisputed fact that early Christians had faith and belief so strong that they were willing to be thrown to the lions rather than renounce their faith in their Lord. These were my grandparents.

It was an epiphany for me. They sat and talked with me and it was weird. It was like they knew but they couldn't have known. But the way they talked and what they said was as though they knew what was happening to me and they let me know that God is watching over me. I had never been able to talk to anyone about what was happening and it was a release of emotion and fear and anxiety. As though they pierced my soul and all the toxic stuff came oozing out and what remained was peaceful and serene. God loves me and he is always there for me and will always be there to listen. All prayers are answered. No matter what was happening around me, no matter how bad it got or how much it changed, he was there. God could be counted upon, always, and there are no circumstances in which God will not know who I am. And best of all, no one could ever take my faith away from me. It seemed to me that almost everything I had ever had or wanted had been taken away from me, but now I had something I could count on that would be mine forever: Faith. And faith, I was told, equaled Love, Gratitude, and Forgiveness. These three things were the tools my grandparents armed me with to get through all the mess that was my life. It was as if they knew what I had kept secret from everyone. And even though things continued to happen that were hard to understand, somewhere deep inside I knew everything would be fine. I began to gain a sense of security and peace because somewhere inside I knew that with God on my side, I could get through anything.

CHAPTER 12

Life from the Control Deck

O*I DON'T THINK YOU CAN RELATE* to how much it meant to me to have a normal life when I went to Florida. It's hard to explain how all those little everyday things brought me joy. I mean seriously, can you imagine getting excited or overwhelmed with happiness because the house was clean? Could you even begin to understand how having three meals a day and clean clothes could all but bring you to tears? For me, having found faith and living in this normal family environment made me feel, for the first time, like a normal kid. I didn't have to take care of anyone or worry about anything most of the time, unless she called, drunk, which she did occasionally, but only occasionally. I began learning Greek, and I could sit for hours listening to my grandparents tell me stories about Greece and when they grew up and how they immigrated to America. Their marriage had been arranged; they literally met on the eve of their wedding. All of it was fascinating to me.

Most of all, I would ask them to tell me about George and Lora, the two people that they knew. I wanted to know them better; I wanted to believe that it wasn't always like this. And I learned that once upon a time, it had been much more normal. They were a typical young couple raising their two boys. Everyone agreed, however, that even in the best of times, George and Lora had a turbulent kind of love—fiery, passionate, but dangerous. It made me sad on a number of levels. It had been there once, it was very important to me that my parents did, in fact, love each other. By all accounts they did, fervently, but it was sad to see from where they started how they ended up. And then it gave me a kind of longing, a sort of melancholy feeling that I had missed out on something special. And while it made me sad on one level, it helped me to love them and forgive them and to be grateful for the blessings I did have in my life.

I stayed all summer away from home and was never homesick for a single day. But then the summer ended and I had to go back, I cried all the way home on the plane.

Over the next several years my life went from one extreme to the other. As my father settled into a relationship with Barb, he became more stable. Weekends with the two of them were drama free and fun. Barb had never married and had no children and she quickly became a friend to me. Mostly, I remember having fun with her and my dad.

On parallel tracks, as life with my father gradually began to improve, life at home was deteriorating at a more rapid speed. And they were still at war so I had to exercise extreme caution about keeping things secret from him so it would not end up in court.

She wasn't always drunk and she worked really hard. Once we moved into the dumpy apartment, she learned to drive and bought an old beat-up car and got a job in a factory. At first she had to work some pretty awful shifts like 11 P.M. to 7 A.M., but after a while she got on the day shift and that was better. When she was sober she was intelligent and funny and you just wanted to be with her, everyone did. In those early years she took in other people's laundry and would iron their clothes to get extra money. My father claimed to be broke and so he was always behind on his child support payments, if he made them at all, although he managed to still drive Lincoln Continentals and live in places much nicer than our dump.

This meant that we were living constantly on the edge. I was always afraid we would get evicted. It didn't help that my mother had never had a checkbook or managed finances so she would blow through her paycheck. That's why I took over balancing the checkbook and writing out the bills. Much of what I learned in those years was about crisis management and taking control. These would become valuable tools that would help me survive my childhood and marketable skills in my career. However, they would also be destructive and crippling when I became a husband and a father.

You have all accused me of being a control freak, which I admit to, and while I don't know that I can ever be cured, I do think I can be in recovery. It's not an excuse. It is a fact that I had to take control from a very young age. I simply had to apply those skills to control outcomes and avoid disasters.

Chapter 13

Have Yourself a Merry Little Christmas

It was Christmas and my mother was having Christmas Eve. By this time, both Nick and Peter had moved out so I was alone with my mom. Knowing how unreliable she was and fearing a potential disaster, as Christmas approached I started preparations early that year. We bought the tree and I decorated as my mom sat and watched, rewarding herself with a case of beer and a pack or two of cigarettes. I had also made sure that she did the Christmas shopping Saturday afternoon since she usually didn't start drinking that early. The night before Christmas Eve we went grocery shopping and I insisted that she prep all the food. She always worked Christmas Eve day so I wanted everything ready to go. The presents weren't wrapped and under the tree but she said she would take care of that when she got home and with everything prepped I knew she would have enough time before my brothers came. I was home from school and talked to her a couple times during the day just to check in and make sure everything would be fine.

I should add that at this juncture, anything could happen. The holiday could be a beautiful and memorable event, full of warmth, excellent food—a great family get-together. Sometimes it happened that way. But a few years earlier, when my brother Peter was still living at home, she came home drunk and ran into a car in the parking lot. We were confronted on Christmas Eve by the landlord and eventually a police officer. She was positively indignant with the police officer rambling on about how the car was parked in her spot as though that, alone, gave her the right to demolish it. As she staggered through her explanation, slurring her words, her two sons stood in the doorway. Making matters worse was the fact that drinking brought out her anger, and she loved nothing better when she was drunk than to start a fight. This was why the landlord had called the cops, and now she was arguing with him. It was humiliating. I think the only reason she wasn't taken down to jail is that the cop felt sorry for my brother and me. I wanted to die, it was bad enough she ruined Christmas but worse, we were exposed. These things were never supposed to be seen or talked about.

"Look, lady, why don't go take a nap and try to sleep it off so you can salvage some of Christmas for your boys." He looked at her as though seeing something gruesome that the dog had thrown up. Then he turned and walked away.

Then again, the next few Christmases were fabulous. So as I waited for her to come home, I wondered which Christmas this one would be, which mother would show up. She only worked half-days on Christmas Eve and as the afternoon stretched on, I knew she had gone out for happy hour. This was never a good sign, it meant the best I could hope for was semi-functional and enough time and coffee to sober up before the boys arrived. The hours stretched out until early evening. When she finally showed up and staggered in, I knew we were facing a crisis. My brothers were due over in less than two hours. If they found out, then my dad would find out and this would end up in court. I had to do something to make sure that didn't happen. Presents weren't wrapped, dinner was not started, and Mom was passed out on the couch. I was panicked and I tried to wake her but she was out cold. I sat in the kitchen looking at her in the darkened living room as she snored on the couch, the lights of the tree and the Christmas music mocking me.

"Merry Christmas."

"I hate you."

"I hate my life."

I suppose there were a lot of things a twelve-year-old could have done at that moment. But I did what you would expect Phill to do. I started the oven and put in the roast. I prepared the other dishes and put them on the stove. Then I set the table and decorated it with holiday favors. Within an hour the place was warm and festive and smelled wonderful, just like Christmas should.

I didn't try to wake her up, it would be touch-and-go but two hours' sleep might be enough for her to get up and rally. I'd seen her get completely loaded and sleep a couple hours and get up like she hadn't had a drop and start all over again. I was praying this would be one of those times.

I had just enough time to make sure there were presents wrapped under the tree. This was the hardest part for me and it still bothers me if I let it. The other stuff was done on autopilot; I simply went through the motions. I actually felt a sense of accomplishment and I began to get cautiously optimistic that we might just avoid a disaster. But as I got out the wrapping paper and pulled the presents out of the shopping bags, I started crying. I mean, I completely broke down. In that moment, I was abruptly and unexpectedly twelve years old. I was done, I didn't want to see my presents let alone wrap them. Suddenly I didn't want any of it, I didn't want to make Christmas, I didn't want to make sure everyone else got to live their lives the way they wanted and leave picking up the shit to me. She got to go out drinking, they got to move away, and I was left to clean up. I hated all of them, I resented all of them, and I was tired. I felt more tired than I had ever been. And every minute that I wasted crying was one less minute I had to clean up this mess.

"Wake up, now, it's Christmas and you have to get up this minute."

"What, what's going on, why are you shouting at me?"

"Mom, it's Christmas, you came home drunk and passed out and Nick and Peter are going to be here any minute."

"Oh my God, I've got to start dinner."

"It's already started, in fact, it's almost done. I just have to mash the potatoes. Get dressed."

"Keep them out here while I wrap the presents."

"It's done."

"What?"

"I said it's done. Now go get dressed."

"Oh, Phillip, you wrapped your own presents?"

"You didn't exactly leave me a lot of choices."

"I'm such a horrible mother."

"Don't start crying, just get dressed, please . . . and Mom, thanks, I really like everything you got me, I mean that."

It was a nice Christmas for them; she pulled it off. They never would have guessed the condition she came home in and the night was flawless. They all enjoyed the evening very much. It still makes me cry.

CHAPTER 14

My Year of Living Dangerously

ALL YEAR LONG I WOULD WAIT for school to end so that I could escape to Florida. I always left the next day after school ended. I could feel myself transforming as the plane took off, leaving all my worries and problems behind me. It freed my mind and lifted my soul. It gave me the ability to regenerate. In later years, after I was no longer able to spend an entire summer, I would seek other, more self-destructive ways to get that same feeling of relief, others means of escape.

It was like living two entirely different, separate lives. It was strange, but this was normal. The school year was tough but I don't how any kid could have had a better life than me during the summers. Summers were a happy time. I got to do all kinds of kid stuff and I never had to clean up any messes. Our family was close, and everyone always made time to stop in or have dinner together and everyone talked to everyone each day. Now we're Greek, so it wasn't completely drama free. There was the time Aunt Stam made a comment about Tiner and they didn't speak for over a year. Actually, during most years someone was not speaking to someone else over something. But I accepted that, and I loved their eccentricities as much as their seemingly normal way of life. Besides, it always passed eventually. I bonded with my cousins, Nicky, Jimmy, and especially my cousin Mary, and we were more like siblings than cousins. I had never been close to my brothers and

I welcomed the connection, it is what I had always wanted with my own brothers.

This was normal. This was a happy family. This is what I had longed for all my life. I never wanted summers to end and I wished I could stay and live with them. The great thing about my childhood is I got to see both sides of the spectrum. I got to see firsthand how things should be, what was "normal" and what was wrong and horrible. At home, there was neglect and abuse; this helped me to formulate what I wouldn't do to my children. I was embarrassed and ashamed of my family. However, I was also living with family members who were everything I thought a real family should be.

This had a profound effect on many of the choices I made as an adult. I refused to admit I was gay, or even consider the possibility. Gay was not normal. I'd spend my entire childhood yearning for something that was always out of my reach, impossible for me to have, a "normal" childhood, family life. I was determined to do something that would wipe out my past. There was no way, as an adult, that I was going to allow myself to explore those feeling. No way would I choose to be "queer." I was determined to take things into my own hands and build a "normal" life for me, a wife, and our children. And, I would gladly have traded sexual satisfaction, intimacy, and even being "in love" for a normal life. When I was growing up, men didn't marry men. No one I knew had two moms or two dads. Being gay meant shaming my family, and certainly never having children or a family of my own. I wanted children; I wanted a family that no one could take away from me. I wanted to fit in. I never let even my closest friends know the truth. Before I hit adolescence, I grew up feeling like a freak. You can't imagine how a questionable sexuality hit me when my hormones started to kick in.

Then one summer, while I was away in Florida, my mom did something that changed our lives dramatically and I, in turn, made some of the worst choices of my life. It was also the year of her second suicide attempt. It was the year I started smoking, got drunk for the first time, had sex with a girl for the first time, started driving a car, inhaled paint thinner, smoked pot, and took several LSD "trips."

I was thirteen years old and starting 8th grade.

Chapter 15

Suicide, the Sequel

OSHE MEANT WELL, SHE REALLY DID. She just didn't have very good child-raising instincts. It was the summer between seventh and eighth grade. I was enjoying another carefree, "normal," summer vacation with my family. While I was down in Florida, my mother packed us up and moved us out of our dumpy little apartment in Golden Valley and into an apartment in New Hope. This was another example of her determination. I didn't know anything about it, she simply packed up our things and moved us and literally told me when she picked me up at the airport. But it was also a good example of just how poor her instinct and judgment was when it came to anything related to raising a child.

The apartment in Golden Valley was a dump, but it was our dump. I was attending school with the kids and friends that I had known since kindergarten. This new apartment complex was nicer; it had garages, the apartments had a dishwasher and a garbage disposal, and in the center of the complex there was a pool and a party room. The reason we could afford to live in this much nicer apartment complex is because my mother and one of her drinking friends, Lucille, decided that since they were both single mothers with one child left at home they would move in together and share a two-bedroom apartment. It was the proverbial accident waiting to happen.

And so when my mother picked me up at the airport that Labor Day weekend just days before schools was starting she told me she had a surprise for me.

"What kind of surprise?"

"You'll see."

"Wait a minute, where we going?"

"That's the surprise."

"You mean we're not going home?"

"Yes, we are going home. We are going to our new home. Wait till you see the new apartment."

"Mom, wait a minute, we moved?"

"Yes, we moved and you're going to love it. It's a beautiful apartment, much nicer than our ghetto apartment."

"Mom, but it's in Golden Valley, right?"

"No, it's in new Hope."

"But I still get to go to school in Golden Valley, right?"

"No, you're starting at a new school, I already registered you."

"Mom, why didn't you tell me? Why didn't we talk about this? We can't afford our apartment in Golden Valley, how are we going to afford something that's even nicer?"

"Because we're sharing the two-bedroom apartment with Lucille and her son Bill."

"How could you do this to me?"

"I thought you would be happy, I'm trying to have a nicer home for us. I guess I can't do anything right."

"No, it's fine. I just wish you had talked to me about it. That's a big deal to have to move and go to a different school. It'll be fine, I'm sure I'll love it."

I hated it. Yes, it was nicer but living with another family in a small two-bedroom apartment? There are no excuses for the poor judgments and really bad decisions I made that year but you have to understand the environment that provided all the right ingredients for disaster.

To begin with, I started out rebellious and resentful. I felt like I'd been tricked. I was used to having far more influence on decisions than any kid my age should have but nevertheless I did, and to not be consulted on this was leaving me angry and spiteful. Yet another example of how things got taken away from me, my home, my friends, my school.

Then there was Lucille. The only thing I knew about Lucille is that she could drink as much as my mother and I couldn't recall ever seeing her sober. Remember, I was used to caretaking and enabling my mom. I monitored her drinking and tried to keep her from harming herself or losing her job; having a drinking buddy as a roommate was going to make my job especially difficult. To make matters worse, Mom had met a couple upstairs, self-proclaimed "hill-billies" from Kentucky who drank cases of beer every night. He was a high school dropout who worked two jobs as a security guard; she was toothless and did not wear dentures, but those gums were as callused and hard as stone and she would bite through cashews and eat corn on the cob. Hank and Alma, naturally they became my mom's best friends and we began spending time in their apartment where they could drink every night.

Hank and Alma had three children and the middle boy was my age and went to my new school. His older sister and her boyfriend were drug dealers and it was through them that I got to purchase Mescaline, Pink Barrels, and Paper Acid, all various forms of LSD. I had tried pot but it failed to have any effect on me so skipping right to the harder stuff seemed appealing, especially since I had spent so many nights hanging out with them when they were all tripping.

I am a parent, it would have taken me minutes to assess the situation and determine that this was not a good environment for my child. But she didn't think that way, at least she never did with me. Despite everything I'm describing, she was actually a wise and loving parent. Her advice was sought after by my friends and even other parents. She just didn't know how to take care of a child. By thirteen, my mom treated me as an adult. Our roles had always been reversed but thirteen was a watershed year in that she seemed to have decided that thirteen was the age of manhood. She had always talked to me like I was an adult, but now she didn't even bother to try to look after me. I started smoking, and she knew it. She just figured I was old enough to make my own decision. And now when we went out to her friends, I was brought along as the designated driver. I was thirteen and driving my mother home after she got too drunk. If I wanted to go over to a friend's, rather than have the burden of dropping her child off and picking him up, she merely threw me the car keys and told me to take the car.

Had she looked at the world through the eyes of a parent who is raising a child entering adolescence, she would've assessed the situation in a far different way and made much better choices. She knew, for example, that I was hanging out with Lucille's son and a group of friends who were older kids in high school. She thought nothing of this. She would spend time in Hank and Alma's apartment at night drinking cases of beer while a steady stream of teenagers would come in and out of the apartment after spending a few minutes in the back bedroom. You don't have to be a drug dealer to be suspicious about that kind of behavior. And by the way, if your thirteen-year-old child is back there, this should cause a parent to be even more alert.

She was entering the really rough years of her life. Stuck with one child left to raise, and a job in a factory where the only way to earn more money was to work overtime and weekends. Her friends were all drinking pals. She was lonely, unhappy, depressed and drinking heavily. The situation with Lucille lasted only a few months and by December 1, she moved me into a one-bedroom basement level apartment in the same complex. The bottom floors were always the cheapest, but it meant she had to routinely work overtime in order to pay the rent. Their divorce became final this year and within months my father remarried Barbara. Although he was more than $10,000 behind in child support payments, he managed to buy her a beautiful diamond ring and they subsequently moved into a very lovely home in an affluent suburb.

I continued to take care of the household responsibilities making sure that the house got cleaned and that the bills got paid but I began wanting more and more to escape. I felt trapped in the life that I didn't want to be in. My brothers were gone, they had escaped. My father and his new bride were living in a wonderful new home with expensive furniture, new cars, and exciting travel. I was stuck in a place that I didn't want to be in, in a school that I hated, and with a group of friends that I know I wouldn't want my children to hang out with.

My mother went out more frequently and I was always alone on weekends. I would often go over to Dad and Barb's. I genuinely wanted to spend time with them, but mostly I just didn't want to be alone. One night, my friend and I went to a party with the older kids and they thought it was funny to get these two thirteen-year-olds drunk. The New Hope water tower was right outside my bedroom window and it had a flashing light on top of it. That night when I got drunk for the first time we staggered down the streets and through the neighborhood toward the flashing red light. I didn't worry at all about getting caught drinking because I knew my mother would either not be back from the bars yet or she would've come home and she would be passed out.

And so the year went. I kept making more and more bad decisions, experimenting and escaping, at every opportunity I could find. And at this point, my whole life was an opportunity to do anything I wanted. One day a girl came over to my apartment, of course I was alone and unsupervised—my mother was working that Saturday. She brought in a can of paint thinner in some plastic bags. She proceeded to put paint thinner in the bag and then put the bag around her nose and mouth and inhale. Each time she would do this she would get an immediate rush and laugh hysterically. She told me to try it and I did. Once we were both high, she told me she wanted to have sex for the first time with me. And we did.

This time it was spring. I knew that she was angry, and she vented her anger toward me when she got drunk. I guess she felt I was just another example of how unfair life was to her. The older boys were gone, George was off with his new wife, she was working long hours and still getting into greater and greater debt. On top of all this, she was stuck having to take care of a thirteen-year-old child. One day I came home after school and there was a note on the kitchen table. It was Thursday and she hadn't gone to work. It was a suicide note to me and it was full of anger and bitterness. I didn't know what to do, my heart started racing and I could feel the panic building up in me, making it difficult to breathe, even to think. I immediately went over and picked up the phone to call the police, and then I hung up. My mind raced through the whole sequence of events and consequences that would occur once the police were called in. In my mind, I thought it meant that this would quickly get out of hand, something that I could no longer control, something that could easily blow up. They might find her, and if they did and she was alive, something would happen to her, I just wasn't sure what. Would she go to jail? Would she be taken to a mental ward in a hospital? Would she lose her job, would we be forced out of the apartment? Would she hate me and resent me forever?

I knew I couldn't call the police. I wasn't sure what else to do but I was certain I couldn't do that. I decided to go out to the garage. Years before her good friend Mrs. Magnusson left a suicide note and went out to the car in the garage and killed herself. It would be a fairly unoriginal way for her to do it, and therefore unlikely, but possible nevertheless. Going out of the apartment that day and over to our garage was one of the longest, hardest walks I've ever taken. I stared at the door of the garage as I approached. When I reached down to turn the handle, I was shaking. I pulled the garage door up and braced myself for what I might see—my dead mother in the car.

The garage was empty. However she intended to end her life, she planned to do it somewhere away from home. In her note to me she said to expect a call when they find her body. I went back into the house and sat down at the table and reread the note to see if there were any clues, anything that would help me know what she was planning to do. I couldn't call my brothers, and I definitely could not call my father. I did call a few of her close friends.

"Hello, Sarah, it's Phill."

"Hi, honey, how are you, is everything all right?"

"Yeah, everything's fine. I was just wondering, is Mom over there?"

"No, she's not."

"Oh, well, have you seen her or talked to her today?"

"No, is she not home from work yet? Maybe she's working late or, you know, maybe she went out with some friends. Don't worry, honey, I'm sure she's fine."

"You're right, she's probably just out with friends. No big deal, thanks, Sarah."

There was nothing I could do but wait. That night I went to sleep alone in our apartment and I prayed to God to save her, I prayed that someone would find her and that she would be okay.

The next morning I got up and ran out to see if she was home, but the apartment was empty. I called my dad and asked him if he could pick me up after school so that I could spend the weekend with them. He said he would be there after work and I hung up, got dressed, and went to school.

No one that day suspected anything. Not my friends, not the teachers—to the outside world it was just me and another day. I guess I was lucky to have had years of training and conditioning. But inside I was getting more and more frightened. I spent that day at school not knowing if my mother was dead or alive. Not knowing if it any minute someone would come into the classroom and take me by the hand and bring me down to the office where police officers would be telling me that her body washed up or it was found in an alley. After school my dad picked me up and I spent the weekend with him. I knew I couldn't possibly sit alone in the apartment waiting to see how everything turned out.

Those four days were hell. It probably seems strange to you that I didn't turn to someone in my family or call the police but you would have to understand what it was like for me at that stage of my life living with my mother. I didn't believe it. Of course it was possible, anything was possible with her, but it was just as possible that she would come back. You just never knew with her. Besides if she was dead she was dead, they would find her and nothing I could say to anyone would make any difference. I thought she's either already dead or she'll come back. I had destroyed the note, I burned it outside of the apartment. It would be yet another one of my secrets, something I intended to take to my grave, and even if she followed through with it and they found her and brought her body to the morgue, no one would ever know about that note, I had made sure of that. On Sunday, my father dropped me off as usual outside of the apartment and I walked slowly through the entryway. I waited outside the door of our apartment. I had run out of time. If she wasn't there, I had to call the police.

She was there, sitting at the table sobbing, dirty, and drunk.

I was so overcome with these intense and powerful conflicting emotions that I literally thought my head was going to explode. I was relieved. I thought she could be dead. I was angry, I wanted to grab her by the throat and shake her and say, "Do you understand what you just put me through?" I wanted to slap her and shout, "Grow up, be responsible, if you can't take care of me at least take care of yourself, I'm tired." And at the same time I wanted to hug her and tell her how much I loved her and how important she is to me. I felt profoundly sorry that she could feel so low and so bad about herself that she would want to take her own life. I just walked up quietly to the table pulled out a chair opposite her, and sat down.

"GO AWAY, LEAVE ME ALONE."

"I'm not going anywhere. Do you know, do you have any idea what the last four days have been like for me, Mom? You left me that note practically blaming me for everything that was wrong in your life. You tell me you're going to kill yourself, and that when they find your body they will let me know. I think you owe me an explanation."

She lifted her head up from the towel that she had been crying in and stared at me for a long time through her glazed and swollen eyes. Without saying a word she got up, walked around me and got herself a bottle of beer. She came back to the table and she sat down and told me her story.

"I'm sorry that I put you through all of this but it's been a rough four days for me as well. I meant to do it, I planned out when and how and where. I wanted it to be quick and it was important to me that my body could be found because I wanted you to have closure.

"But why, Mom?"

"Because I just didn't think I had any reason to live. I'm disgusted at what I've done with my life. I love you, Phillip, and look what I'm doing to you. I don't deserve to be your mother and you don't deserve to have me as a mother. I left here and I drove down to a bridge over the Mississippi. I waited till the middle of the night and I got out of the car and I walked over and I got up on the edge of the bridge. I wasn't scared, it was serene, really very peaceful. The water below was dark and still and I could see the reflection of the moon in the water. All in all it was a beautiful evening and I thought a beautiful way to leave this world behind. Then two men under the bridge on the side of the embankment called out to me. Had they waited another 30 seconds, it would've been over. But it disrupted the harmony of the moment and I certainly didn't want an audience. The sound of their voices and the sight of them standing there waving to me brought me back from a very deep, almost trance-like state of mind, and back into this reality of the world and all the pain and suffering that goes along with it. I climbed back down off the ledge and found my way down to where they were. That's where I've been for four days. They saved me and I think they were there for a purpose."

"I love you, Mom."

"I love you too, Phillip."

I never learned anything more about those two men or how they spent the four days together. I don't believe in coincidences, I think God was watching over her and I think she was right, they were there for a reason. We never spoke about it again and I never told anyone.

Chapter 16

Denial

I DON'T KNOW IF I WAS EVER A KID. It never felt like I was. I always kind of knew more than any of the kids my age. I was in awe of their confidence and their comfort. I pretended, as best I could, to be the same. And so, I began honing my acting skills at an early age. I could assimilate normal so well that no one in the outside world had any clue. That's how I pulled it off. And it wasn't just the acting normal for people to see, it was the internal part, the inside of me that was not visible to anyone but me: my mind, my emotions, my psyche. I learned how to take a thought or a fear and lock it away. The combination of these survival skills got me through the life I felt I was stuck in. Without them, I could never have gotten through that weekend. If I had for a moment let my thoughts and fear turn to "what if . . ." I would have gone over the edge. I literally had to hold out not just for practical reasons but for my sanity as well.

This skill, or disability, depending on how you look at it, got me through those four days. Years later it would get me through the horrible week when mom died, and the week after that when I woke up and the house was on fire.

I know that it is hard to believe or understand that I "didn't know" I was gay. You asked me, "How come you didn't figure it out earlier?" It's not like I was clueless, I realized as I hit puberty that I found males attractive, and it frightened me. These things were put inside an impenetrable chest and buried in a deep, dark place. These things were never processed; they never saw the light of day. And over the years, they brewed and festered, locked away in the dark recesses of my mind. In my attempt to control them they were really controlling me. But my life up to this point had been like a training camp for how to control, how to avoid, how to pretend. I found men attractive but I also found women attractive and there simply was no choice in my mind. I have known many alcoholics, and they all have one thing in common—denial. Even those who have been sober for years will tell you that before they hit their bottom, they refused to believe that they were powerless over alcohol, even after they lost their spouse, their job, their house, their money. That is how powerful denial can be.

My thoughts about my sexuality were too disturbing for me to even take out and examine and I would never have talked to anyone about them. But that's what I was good at; keeping it to myself, controlling the environment and acting "as if..."

As if my family was just like everyone else's.

As if I had a great time trick-or-treating at my cousin's.

As if my mother didn't try to do it, it was an accident.

As if everything at home was fine and it was just another day at school.

As if Christmas was ready to go.

As if my heart wasn't breaking.

As a teenager, it made me angry to have confusing and conflicting thoughts about sex. Thank you, God, just what I needed, one more way to be different; another giant step from being like everybody else. Thank you, God, may I have another? By the time I hit my twenties, I had neatly organized and rationalized the topic: I was bisexual, I read up on it and this became my rational. Some people, for unknown reasons, are attracted to both men and women.

The American Psychological Association states that "sexual orientation falls along a continuum. In other words, someone does not have to be exclusively homosexual or heterosexual, but can feel varying degrees of both."

That was it, I had found my excuse. It was no one's business but my own and since I never acted on it, I simply locked it away.

Not that it justifies anything I did, but there is only one person (at that time) that I ever told this to and that was your mother before we got married. I told her truthfully that I was attracted, sexually, to women but that I found men attractive as well and that I had never acted on that but I wanted her to know in case she didn't want to marry me. I told her I was not gay and that is exactly what I made myself believe at the time. I was as honest with her as I was with myself.

Chapter 17

Everyone?

SO I ENDED MY THIRTEENTH YEAR with a bad LSD trip that took 72 hours for me to come down. I cannot even describe how frightening it is to feel as though you have lost your sanity, and as I look back now I feel tremendously sad for this fucked-up thirteen-year-old child/man. A mother, a father, a stepmother, two brothers, and no one saw anything or suspected anything? How is it that all those things happened to a thirteen-year-old kid? I knew where you kids were virtually every minute of the day and night when you were thirteen. Don't get me wrong, it was my fault, they were my decisions but you have to ask yourself how accountable is a thirteen-year-old child? Christ, if you give a child a blowtorch, can you really get angry if they burn down the barn? At the end of that year, I looked back at my life and the choices I had made and the consequences that I had suffered, and I realized that I really had always been responsible for my own wellbeing. This was a hard lesson but a wakeup call, nonetheless. We all decided a break would be in order and I went to live with Dad and Barb.

It was what I needed. The house was clean, we ate three meals, I would come home after school and Barb would be baking cookies. I dove into schoolwork and for the first time in my life I was a straight-A student. It gave me a new start. For all its outward appearances, we were a happy, normal family just like everyone else in the neighborhood. However, my father saw this as his opportunity to "fix" me.

My father could have been the prototype for Professor Higgins in *My Fair Lady*. And while I'm on a theatrical theme, there is a line in a song from *Wicked* where the character sings, "And when someone needs a makeover I simply have to take over, I know, **I know** exactly what they need, follow my lead . . . ." That was George. My dad spent much of his life criticizing and then fixing people. Tear 'em down and build 'em up. Actually he was pretty good at it and oftentimes people came to him, but usually he would initiate the discussion by pointing out someone's flaws. Everyone was fair game—subordinates, friends, family, children. He would tear them down and then offer to help and coach. In fact, many of his friends called him Coach.

And so at fourteen, I became my father's next project. In his usual, straight-forward no-nonsense approach, he sat me down virtually the day I moved in and told me, "Everyone thinks you're queer."

"Everyone?"

"Everyone. Believe me."

"But no one's ever told me that."

"Don't tell me you've never been called a fag. Every time you open your mouth a purse falls out. Look, everyone thinks it or says it behind your back."

"I guess I didn't know that."

"Well, I don't know how you couldn't, it's obvious to everybody. Is that what you want?"

"No."

This, of course, is where he would come in for the kill; his timing was always impeccable. Hard as it may seem to believe, this was actually shocking and very depressing news to me. I never thought of myself as effeminate or "queer." It was a painful blow, but it hit the target and shattered my confidence. All this time, I thought, every time I walk into a room? Fourteen is an awkward age for any young teenager, even for me, and I had many more years of life's experience than the average fourteen-year-old. Nevertheless, that part of my psyche, my ego, was still developmentally like a typical fourteen-year-old kid. I wondered why no one had ever told me, and it hurt me deeply to think that everyone was thinking this behind my back. I would've done anything at that moment to change, and of course, he knew that.

"If you want to change that, I will help you, but you're going to have to do as I say and I'm going to be very straightforward with you. You must not get offended or hurt when I tell you these things because it is all for your own good."

"Yes, of course, I will."

And he was true to his word. He would criticize the way I walked into the room, or the way I used my hands too dramatically when I spoke, or even how I expressed my thoughts or feelings if I was engaged in conversation or told a story.

"There you go again."

"What, what am I doing?"

"It's not what you're doing, it's what you're saying. That's something a girl would say. You should have said, it's the way you look and feel the next day after you got two black eyes."

"Sorry, Dad."

"It's okay, you're actually getting better."

When these things occurred and there were people around, he was nice enough to take me aside in private. But at home, he would blurt things out, then and there, without warning. It was unsettling. I literally never knew when he would attack. The problem was, I really didn't see myself that way, and so I didn't know when I was acting "queer." But just as a dog learns the boundaries when you install Invisible Fencing and put a shock collar around his neck, so did I learn how to adjust my behavior to avoid the painful shock. Slowly, I began to change. I was grateful to him on one level, now that I knew I could add it to the constant list of things I had to hide.

Looking back, I guess I should be grateful; he was probably right. While it did, in fact, make me more aware and objective about my mannerisms and the way in which I expressed myself, it also made me profoundly self-conscious, and this I would carry throughout most of my adult life literally until the day I came out. Never again would I walk into a room or carry on a conversation without caution. Twenty years later, when I was married and had children of my own, I could not engage in a conversation at a neighborhood party without being self-conscious about everyone thinking that I was gay. And of course, despite my best efforts, everyone did think I was gay. My coming-out was a non-event. Other than Itsie, anyone I ever told was like "Yeah, I knew that, so what was this big thing you wanted to tell me?"

"That was the big thing, I'm gay."

"Well, I always thought you were. What took you so long to figure it out?"

Nevertheless, I kept at it all those years. I learned how to pretend I was interested in sports. I avoided joining in on conversations that women might bring up on topics such as decorating or types of colors (I pretended not to know what taupe was). But mostly, through all those years, I felt like I didn't fit in. And that was because I didn't, I was "acting as if . . . ." Years later, when I had this beautiful wife and four wonderful children and I became a successful executive, I used all of those things to shield my discomfort and self-consciousness. I may not have known sports, but I could talk kids and business with the best of them.

Overall, staying with my dad and Barb was a good experience and after my previous year, probably the best choice considering my options. They were very nice to me and they created a home environment where I even felt comfortable spontaneously bringing friends over to just hang out. It gave me a year to recharge and although I spent almost every weekend at my mom's, the burden of caring for her was greatly lessened just due to the amount of time that I was away from her.

However, I was a guest. That was made clear to me. This was Barb's home, and this was their life, and by the end of my ninth-grade year I began to feel like the houseguest that wouldn't leave. Everything was theirs, it belonged to them, even the things they got for me. By spring, I had outgrown a pair of jeans they had bought me when I started school so I cut them off to wear as shorts. Barb was furious. She admonished me and told me they had bought the clothes and they were to be returned to her when I would no longer needed them; she had nephews she planned to give them to. The furniture we picked out for my bedroom was theirs and it stayed with them. I got to use it, just as other guests in their home.

Chapter 18

Home Alone

After a year of repose, I packed up and moved back home with my mom. She agreed to rent an apartment back in Golden Valley so I would rejoin my friends and school. I felt rested and Dad and Barb were very understanding, I think relieved. A year had made a big difference, I was fifteen now and growing into the adult that I had always been to her. For one thing, I needed less care, and like all teenagers, I wanted to be out with my friends, not hanging out with my mom. Gone were the days when I would beg her to take me to a movie or a drive-in. We became more comfortable because I was getting old enough to take care of myself legitimately.

This was where she was at her best parenting. Listening, talking, laughing, relating to one another on an adult level. She was intelligent and wise and gifted with a dry wit that was very funny. Despite her poor parenting instincts raising and caring for children, I would seek her advice and so did most of my friends. These were the years when I was envied as having the coolest mom. And she was to them, but they never saw the side I kept secret. They'd see her have a few drinks but I always managed to get them out of there before it got worse. She started dating again and I didn't feel so lonely anymore because I was out with my friends. Granted it was a little weird to be the only kid without a curfew but I could handle it.

The first year went pretty well. I was happy to be back at my school with my old friends. She found a decent one-bedroom apartment and she slept on the couch. I started working so now I was really becoming more independent. The less I needed her to take care of me, the more I began to appreciate how truly unique and wonderful she was.

By summer, I got my driver's license and started working retail about 20 hours a week, full time in the summer. But as that first year ended, she started dating one guy, Bob. He would eventually become her second husband. At first, she would spend Friday or Saturday night at his place. Soon it became the weekend, and as I entered my sophomore year she had pretty much moved out. I was sixteen and basically had my own apartment. She would occasionally come home one night a week to get clothes.

It's not that I couldn't handle it, I'd been cooking and cleaning and doing laundry for years. It was that I felt abandoned and lonely. And of course, once again, I was left on my own to make whatever choices I wanted without adult supervision or care. And most of those decisions were bad. I was the envy of all my friends, the life of the party, and happy and carefree on the outside; horribly lonely and miserable on the inside. So I escaped.

CHAPTER 19

What Doesn't Kill You, Makes You Stronger

I'VE NEVER HAD MUCH TOLERANCE FOR DRUNKS or drug addicts who fail to take responsibility for their behaviors. The ones who blame their parents, or their circumstances, or even some terrible event that happened to them, for their own poor choices. I have seen people brandish their unfortunate circumstances like a "get out of jail free" card providing an irrevocable excuse that releases them from any personal accountability. I don't believe anyone asks to be an alcoholic or an addict, and I really believe it is genetic; however, treatment is available to anyone. I don't mean that I judge these people, it's just that I can relate to being miserable and unhappy and turning to drugs or alcohol to "self-medicate." That's exactly how I got through the last three years of high school until I was finally free to leave home.

I had spent most of my first fifteen years taking care of a sick parent, worrying about what would happen next, hiding my true thoughts, fears, and feelings. I had seen and experienced many things that no kid should ever be exposed to. By fifteen, I'd had enough. Not that it is true or an excuse but I felt that I had been robbed of a childhood. And because I was young and inexperienced, I believed that all the kids I knew had a "normal" family and life. This was probably not true, but it was my reality. And so I tuned out.

Those years were really strange as I look back on them. It isn't that I didn't have contact with my mom. We talked every day, and we would meet for lunch or go out to dinner, and as I said she did come home occasionally, but there's no question I was living on my own. I could have friends over, I could have parties, I could stay up as late as I wanted and if I didn't feel like going to school I simply stayed home. I missed 36 days of school my senior year. I guess in some ways my circumstances had really gotten much better. I no longer had the burden or responsibility of taking care of my mom and dealing with whatever latest drama she created. And in that way, truthfully, my life was better. I actually had a lot of fun during those years, mostly getting high with friends and partying. But all my friends still lived at home, they had to go to school on time, their mom or dad or both attended the school conferences and there were consequences to deal with if they skipped school or didn't turn in homework. They had curfews, and if they didn't come home on time someone was waiting up for them worried and then relieved to see them home safe. Much as the other kids envied my freedom, I envied their adult supervision. I still had the fantasy—I wanted to be taken to a boarding school or a foster family. I wanted someone to be angry if I broke the rules.

There were no rules. No one was ever waiting up for me, no one was worried if I came home late. No one in my family asked about my schoolwork or talked to my teachers or checked in on me. I would have parties and friends would come over and we would get high and have a few drinks and I could totally escape. It was fun and carefree. But then each of them would have to leave so they could get home on time to avoid getting their car privileges taken away. And I was always left alone. Looking back on it, I'm amazed that no one stepped up to change what was an unacceptable environment for a high school kid. It's not like I wasn't in touch with my family. We would see one another at holidays and birthdays and special occasions, but no one really knew me.

I hope you all look back fondly on your high school years; the highs, the lows, and everything in between. It really is a special time; it is a coming-of-age for all adolescents. I have those fond memories and what was special and distinct about those last few high school years for me is that up to that point in my life I didn't have very many fond memories, and I was certainly never carefree. However, they are nevertheless painful memories at the same time. It saddens me to think that no one cared enough to look in on this teenage boy. Sometime around my junior year I discovered white cross—it's an amphetamine commonly known as speed. What started out as a seemingly innocent way to help me focus and get caught up on homework and housework quickly turned into an increasingly alarming dependence. I would wake up at four in the morning and take a few pills go back to sleep and wait for the onset of action to wake me up. Then throughout the day I would continue taking more each time the effect began to wear off. I lost my appetite and therefore a lot of weight. I began keeping a journal of what I ate noting the date and time after I almost passed out in school. I realized I couldn't remember the last time I had eaten. I mostly lived off hot tea and cigarettes. I was a skinny kid to begin with but my weight dropped alarmingly down to about 95 pounds.

One morning after I took my shower and I was getting ready for school I was frightened at what I saw in the mirror. My hair was falling out, my clothes were baggy and too big, and I looked like shit. I literally started shaking and I couldn't stop. My heart was racing and I thought maybe I had overdosed. I sat down on the couch and I remember saying out loud, "Somebody help me, please, somebody help me." But I was home alone and there was no one there to help me. And then I did what I had often done when I felt alone and abandoned, I got down on my knees and I asked God to help me. I confessed to him all of the things that I had been doing and wept as I confided how scared and sad and alone I felt. And ashamed, I begged for forgiveness. I asked him for the strength and the courage to help me overcome this addiction. I never took another amphetamine again.

Some people letter in sports in high school, others are proud to have been in choir or played in the band. Whatever a person's talent is, most people are proud to look back on one or more of their accomplishments. My greatest accomplishment in high school was beating an addiction to amphetamines.

I can admit now that it took me years to get over the anger and resentment I harbored against my family. My father and my two brothers had escaped, leaving a young child to deal with the troubled and unstable parent. And they should have known better. Everyone knew how unstable she was. No one reached out, no one confronted her, and no one tried to help me. And now as a teenager in high school even my mother had escaped, all of them abandoning me and leaving me to my own devices. But God hadn't abandoned me, and it reinforced what I had known for most of my life—I was responsible for my own wellbeing and God is the only one who always cares, who always listens, and is always there in my hour of need.

They say that what doesn't kill you, makes you stronger. It was the story of my life. By my senior year, I was determined to pull out of the insanity that had been my childhood and family upbringing and to make something of my life. Although I didn't have the grades or the money, I was determined to go to college and be the first member of my family to graduate with a college degree. I began setting goals, not just for school but for what I wanted to accomplish in my life. My childhood sucked, okay. My mom was a mess, my family disconnected and dysfunctional, check and check. I was determined that this would not define who I was or what my future would be.

My mother battled her own demons, but for all the troubled times there is one amazing thing I can say about what she did for me for which I will always be grateful. She made me believe that I could do anything I set out to accomplish. She told me I was special and that I had what most people lack. And above all else, she told me that my brothers and I were the best thing she ever did in life and that she loved us more than life itself. This was not a one-time conversation, I grew up hearing this and believing this all of my life. There were a lot of difficult times in my childhood and adolescence but I never felt unloved, and her absolute unwavering faith in me did, in fact, make me think that I was special.

CHAPTER 20

Senior Year

SO I GOT TO GO TO ENGLAND MY SENIOR YEAR. This was another turning point in my life. Yes, it was really great to visit England, go to school and stay with my host family but most of all it was my first attempt at setting and successfully achieving a goal. Through the years there have been many, but it started there. It was significant on many levels—of course it was fun and a great adventure for a seventeen-year-old kid, but it was so much more than just that. I was pulling myself up and out of the life I hated. I was tired of just escaping and not really accomplishing anything other than a good high and a few laughs. It was a turning point in my life when I made up my mind that the past was behind me and now it was my turn to make something out of my life or not.

Going overseas to England became my first real ambition. Up to that point, I had never really applied myself to anything that was just for me. As a kid, my parents never signed me up for camp, or gave me music lessons; they were completely uninvolved, busy fighting each other and partying. In high school, when I showed up for class and bothered to do schoolwork I usually got an 'A' but this was almost always offset by my repeated absences and failure to turn in other schoolwork. Besides, I was usually stoned. I had never participated in extracurricular activities, although my friend talked me into joining the wrestling team, which I did until got kicked off when I got suspended for smoking. I spent my adolescent years in a complete reversal of the serious, ever-responsible, angst-ridden child that I had been my whole life. And since I was basically living alone, with a family that had always been disconnected from me, it was easy to do. But then I heard about the school organizing a trip to England where we could sign up to go over with our principal, whom I knew very well having spent almost every morning in his office, and I wanted to go. We were to spend a semester in a small village near Peterborough and attend Prince William School in Oundle.

So I signed up. I even went to the afterschool meeting and got all of the paperwork that my parents were supposed to fill out. I was working a lot so I had almost enough money to fund the trip and I got my parents to put up the rest. As the time got closer I could feel myself changing, I was actually engaged in something. I picked up extra shifts, I was careful not to get into trouble at school (anyone attending had to be in "good standing"), and I was actually completing work and following through with all that was required. I had to write a letter to my host family, buy the supplies from the list they provided, purchase my airline ticket and all that. The significance of all this is that for three years I hadn't done much of anything except get stoned and party. Of course, taking on responsibility and getting things done was second nature to me—remember, I was balancing the checkbook when I was ten—but these skills had been lying dormant for years and for the first time I was applying them to something for me that I wanted rather than for taking care of something, or someone, usually to avoid a crisis. This was for me.

I had an amazing time. Somehow I managed to go the whole semester without getting stoned, and I got to experience life in England living with an English family. I actually made up my mind that I would quit smoking pot; I didn't need it, I was having a great time without it. All the other kids went through various degrees of homesickness at first but of course I didn't, it's not like I was used to coming home to a family, I was on my own.

While there, I did build quite a reputation for not exactly getting into trouble, but more or less having trouble somehow find me. Most of the time it wasn't my fault. For example, we were brought on a bus to some new development to tour the city and it culminated with a tour of some of the new suburban homes that were recently built. I think the point was to show us how modern England was because we were all living in a small Elizabethan principality. Anyway, I left the tour group because I was bored and I had to pee so I wandered upstairs and found the bathroom and the next thing I knew I was locked in. The window only opened about six inches or I would have jumped out. Well, you'd think I had committed an act of treason. Everyone started shouting and knocking at the door and telling me to remain calm but try as they might, no one could get the door open and eventually the entire group had to get back on the bus and leave without me. I managed to stick my arm out the window and wave to them as they left to go back. In the end, they got some guy to come and take the door apart, which did nothing to help the developer's mood. Then someone had to drive me back and muttered something about "daft Yanks."

This was the first of many incidences and before long I was assigned my own chaperone. There were three adults traveling with our group along with the principal and his wife and they would trade off on who would shadow me. I still managed to lose them, which I did mostly out of spite.

But all good things come to an end and when the semester ended and it was time to leave I was really sad. Everyone else was ready to get back home because everyone else had a life they wanted to get back to. I didn't want to leave.

We all boarded the plane and made the eight-hour flight back to Minnesota. When we arrived, all the parents and some of the siblings were waiting at the baggage claim for us. Some of them had homemade signs welcoming their child back, others had balloons or flowers. You could tell how much they had missed their kid and almost everyone in our group practically ran into their open arms. It was really touching to see.

No one was there waiting for me.

I was the only one without a parent of family member there to greet me. I had talked to my mom, she had all the flight information she told me she would be there to pick me up. I felt really bad, but worse than that I felt embarrassed. The other kids and even their parents were concerned and asking if I needed a ride. I just kept telling them everything was fine but you could tell by the looks on their faces that they felt sorry for me. Welcome back to my life. Just after the last of them had gone and I was sitting alone with my bags I saw them, well, actually I heard them first. My mother and Bob came staggering around the corner, they were drunk and loud and at that moment I was actually glad they hadn't been there on time. I would have hated for the other kids and their normal families and parents to have witnessed that. I hated her then, just as I had so many other times she or my dad let me down. I thought, *Really, it meant more to you to go out and get drunk than to see me after I've been gone for three months?* They insisted on taking me out to dinner and I barely spoke and didn't eat anything, I just wanted to get away from them and my life so I told them to just take me home. They dropped me off and went back to his place and I spent my first night back getting stoned, by myself, wondering what all the others were doing tonight. Comparing my experience to what I assumed was theirs.

They had parents who had taken the time to make signs and buy balloons. They had parents who had showed up on time and greeted them like they were special and missed. I hated all of them and that night I actually cried myself to sleep.

Although it hadn't ended on a good note, the trip to England was nevertheless a highlight and a changing point. All those skills I learned for survival could be put to good use. I could get things done. None of the other kids who had gone had done much more than write a letter to their host families; their parents had done all the rest. I had filled out all the forms, organized what needed to be done and figured out all the timing and requirements. I had set a goal to go to England and with little help or guidance, I achieved it. I was determined to control my life and not be controlled by it. Next I set my sights on going away to college. I wanted to make something out of my life—I wanted to travel, I wanted to make enough money to have my own independence and live the way I wanted. Since I didn't have any aptitude to learn a trade, I knew I would need a degree to get to where I wanted to go.

Unfortunately, this decision came to me too late. I returned home from England in April of my senior year. By this time everyone who was going to college had taken the required exams, applied at various schools and were awaiting the outcomes. I hadn't studied for or taken any college entrance exams and at present, I was maintaining a D+ grade average. I wasn't even sure if I was going to graduate. The odds were clearly against me. I cursed myself for waiting until the last moment to figure this out. But I have never been easily intimidated, thanks to my parents and the upbringing (or lack thereof) they provided, so I just ignored the odds and began to figure out how this could be done despite my grades and general lack of preparedness for further education.

"It can't," Mr. Flolid said.

"It can't what?" I asked, sitting across from him in his office, where I had spent so much time during the last three years.

"It can't be done. Period. You've done little to prepare yourself during your tenure at high school for a life of a college student. You're not college material, Mr. Williams. Learn a trade. Dunwoody would accept your application, higher institutes of academic study will not."

"Why am I not college material, Mr. Flolid?"

"Where do I begin, Mr. Williams? You've missed 31 days of school your senior year, you're graduating, if you graduate, in the bottom 10% of your class. By the way, do you know if you are graduating?"

"No, it depends on Simonson, and if he gives me a D- I graduate, if it's an F, I don't."

"There you have it, do I need to go on? Do you really need convincing? You haven't taken any college entrance exams. You must be realistic about your life choices from here. Go out and get a job or learn a trade and grow up."

I thanked Mr. Flolid for his sound advice and told him he was wrong. I was going to college and furthermore, I would make something out of my life. Mr. Flolid's lecture did not have his intended effect on me. Where he had hoped to discourage any delusional thoughts I had of going to college, he had succeeded only in pissing me off, and I'm always at my most determined best when someone tells me I can't do something.

So graduation night I went out with friends and drank and showed up for the ceremony just a little buzzed. Everyone was asking if I graduated and I told them, honestly, that I wasn't sure and that Simonson's grade would be the deciding factor. My father was there with my uncle and my mom brought Bob.

I looked up and my dad waved to me. I thought, *Oh, shit, this would be the one event you'd show up for.* I knew it going to be awkward if they skipped over my name and everyone else went up to get their diplomas. For once, I was actually hoping they were drunk.

Thankfully, Phill Williams was, in fact, called to come up and receive his diploma. The entire graduating class of 1975 stood up and started clapping and hollering. My father, to his dying day, loved to tell the story of how I was the only kid in my class to graduate with a standing ovation that he assumed was due to my popularity.

Chapter 21

UMD

As you know, I did go to college, I did successfully enter into a career, and in fact, I managed to get two master's degrees while running commercial operations and raising my kids as a single parent in joint custody with your mother after our divorce. My childhood may not have been a happy one but it did provide me with a valuable education. I was tough, I could survive, and I could get things done.

However, it was a rocky start, at best. I was determined and I had been told it wasn't possible, so that helped. I did some research and found that the University of Minnesota in Duluth had a "general college" program that accepted virtually any applicant and placed the student on immediate probation. Special classes were offered and maintaining a minimum grade point average was required, but other than that, it was just like any other student at the school. I applied and was accepted, and while I had never visited the school, that fall my mother and Bob, whom she had married, drove me up and dropped me off. I couldn't recall ever being so happy.

Three really great things came out of my move to Duluth. First, I had escaped. I left the life I hated behind (or so I thought); second, I excelled at school and learned how to apply the discipline needed to succeed in college. And finally, I met Susan, who became my dear friend and helped change my life. And although UMD only lasted two years, it was pivotal in the developments that would shape many of the choices I was to make as an adult.

Back at home, things were going from bad to worse. Bob was a raging alcoholic and my mother started drinking at an even more alarming rate than I had ever seen previously. When I was home for the weekend I would stay at their apartment and by the time I got out of bed on Saturday morning they were both stinking drunk. They had developed a pattern of waking up around 5 A.M. to start drinking. By noon they were smashed. They would then go to bed to sleep it off for a few hours and wake up and repeat the whole thing.

But this actually wasn't the worst of it, for Bob had a very violent and abusive side that began to come out during these rages. She would drunk dial her kids and tell us that Bob had given her a black eye or knocked her down. But once she'd sobered up and we asked her about it she denied everything and said she didn't recall even saying that. Then she'd have a brunch or a beautiful family dinner at their place and act as if nothing had happened. We all talked about it and the general thought was that she must be making it up until finally one weekend I came face to face with the truth.

CHAPTER 22

Guilt

ONE OF THE CASUALTIES OF BEING RAISED by an alcoholic parent is the lasting effect of enormous feelings of guilt. Guilt you put upon yourself and guilt the alcoholics thrust upon you to alleviate their own thoughts of guilt and self-loathing. It is horrible and crippling and undeserved. It is easy to blame yourself for something they did. Those terrible thoughts of *Maybe if I hadn't done something she wouldn't have gotten drunk* are useless but hard to avoid. And the alcoholic knows this—it's part of the disease. They'll do anything to keep drinking, anything to avoid taking personal responsibility, and a child (at any age) of an alcoholic is easy prey. It took me years of therapy and support groups to shed the tons of weight of useless guilt I carried every day.

It happened one weekend when I was home from school. As usual, I went out with friends and spent as little time at their place as possible. I hated seeing them both get literally "fall-down drunk." On Saturday night I came home late and all the lights were out but in the darkness, by the fireplace, I could see the burning ember of a lit cigarette. It was so dark that it looked as though it was moving back and forth in midair all by itself. I walked into the room and called out, "Mom, is that you?"

There was no answer and the ghost cigarette just kept moving back and forth. Someone inhaled and then exhaled.

"Mom, why are you just sitting in the dark?"

I walked around feeling my way to the end table and turned on a lamp.

She was sitting in a robe and pajamas near the fireplace smoking. She looked up and stared at me. A broken beer bottle lay at her feet.

Blood caked her mouth. You could see where the blood had flowed out of her mouth, down her chin and splattered all over her.

Dried blood. I wondered how long she had been there, waiting for me, not moving. It was so premeditated, she wanted me to have the full effect. I was horrified.

"Did he do this to you? What happened? Are you alright, do you need a doctor?"

She got up slowly and never took hers eyes off of me. She was obviously very drunk but she also had this strange look on her face and an expression of scorn as she walked slowly over to me. She stood right in my face. Finally she just said, "Now you see what I have to go through so that you can go to college."

And with that, she turned and went to bed.

Chapter 23

Shame

SO THERE YOU HAVE IT. It was my fault. My fault she was a drunk, my fault she was in an abusive relationship. My fault for every bad choice she made in her life. When I was little, I somehow believed that it was my fault that my parents didn't get along and broke up. As I entered adolescence, she left me a note blatantly telling me that because of me she had to commit suicide, I'd left her no choice. And now I realized in horror that the "stories" were true. He was beating her, and according to my mother, this, too, was my fault. My repulsion upon making the discovery that this man was actually physically abusing my mother, beating her, was trumped by my shame for being the cause. Cognitively, I knew that it couldn't be my fault but psychologically and emotionally, she had succeeded in making me feel responsible.

All bullshit. However, easy to take on even though I was nineteen and deep down should have known better. Bob and my mom had made some arrangement, her idea not mine, where I would borrow the money for school from Bob with the expectation that I would pay him back upon graduating. I preferred to get student loans but they wouldn't hear of it and actually the times we talked about it they were both sober so I went along with it. Bob and I wrote out a contract and off I went. Perhaps the thought of having his stepson living with them fulltime had something to do with it, a small price to pay to get me out of there. So in her drunken alcoholic state of mind, she had transferred the responsibility to her son and made somewhat of a martyr of herself.

I left in the night and drove back to Duluth. Of course, I told no one. However, I did call both my brothers the next day and told them I knew she was not making it up, I just didn't tell them how I knew.

Chapter 24

The Call

LIKE ALL HORRIBLE CALLS, this one came in the middle of the night. She was drunk, he had beat her up again but this time it was worse. He left her in bad shape and then he simply left and she didn't know where he was but this time she was afraid and wanted to get out before he came back. I told her to pack up and go over to Sarah's and wait for me there. I was careful to ask about the extent of her injuries to see whether she needed to go to an emergency room but she refused and said she would go straight to Sarah's. Mind you, I had classes the next day, homework to do, assignments to turn in, and work, but nothing for me in my life had ever taken priority over taking care of her. I got up and got dressed and drove the three hours that it took to get to her.

It was around 5 A.M. when I got there and she had already called Dr. Warren, the neighbor who had helped her when she slashed her wrist. He had arranged for her to go to St. Mary's so I brought her there, checked her in, and waited.

She was lucky, I guess, in that her injuries could have been much worse. He knocked out a couple of teeth, blackened her eye, but her jaw was not broken, he had only managed to give her a hairline fracture. She was to stay there a few days under Doctor Warren's care. I had to get back to school but they would call me when it was time for her to get released. That would give me a few days to get her a decent lawyer, get her things out of that apartment, and find her a place to stay. Oh, and somehow figure out a way to also keep up with my college work as well.

I talked to her every day and she seemed to actually be in good spirits. She sounded confident and even optimistic. I was impressed with how brave she was. Leaving him meant she literally had nothing. No place to live, no credit, no car, and a future that was completely unknown. But she was employed, she was smart, and she was strong.

Then, out of the blue, she called and told me she had checked herself into a six-week treatment program connected to the hospital to quit drinking. She had hit the bottom, but this time rather than turning to alcohol to escape or worse, she was determined to get sober and make something other than a tragedy of her life.

Chapter 25

A Second Chance

Susan and I had moved in together in the fall. We'd started hanging out my freshman year after she cast me in one of her directing scenes. She was also a theater major and a few years older than me. We became instant best friends. She was smart, generous, kind, and funny as hell. President of her sorority, she was also someone who could succeed at anything she set out to do. She had all the qualities that make up someone immensely popular. You know that guy or that girl, the one that everyone wants to be, everyone likes, the ones who are not stuck up, though they could be, the people who don't seem to realize just how special they are. That would have been Susan, except Susan was overweight and though I thought she was beautiful—in truth, she was plain. And so sadly, too many people never took the opportunity to get to know this beautiful person.

She was also the first person I ever trusted and for that, I will always be grateful. Despite what would happen, despite how much I still miss her, she was my gift from God. At an early age, I figured out you don't tell people the truth if it's really bad. My dad hadn't hit my mom and knocked her out in a drunken rage, she "tripped and fell and hit her head." I learned too young that people will judge you and not like you. Even my closest friends didn't know anything bad about my life, they only knew what I wanted them to know. I made it as normal as I could. So there was never anyone to talk to, no one to whom I could turn to for sympathy, or help, or just to listen. Until Susan.

For the first time I didn't think that if she knew the truth, she wouldn't want to be my friend. I don't know why but it was wonderful. Still, I was careful about what I would reveal but just even being able to scratch the surface was amazing. I told her all about Bob and the truth about what happened to Lora and why she was in the hospital. Susan had met Lora and they had already become friends. When she heard, she called Lora and drove down to see her that weekend. And for the next six weeks we drove down to see Lora while she was in rehab. I was so proud of her and so proud to be her son. At one visit, this young girl came up to me and told me, "Your mother is the best thing that ever happened to me and the reason I'm alive and getting through this, you're so lucky, I wish she was my mom."

It brought out the very best in her and everyone loved her and sought out her advice, even the counselors. It was unquestionably the best time of my life. She was so brave, she had a job but that was it. We got her an attorney and moved her stuff into storage. No credit, no money, no security, but she was Lora and she knew she could do anything she set her mind to do. And now, for the first time I could ever remember, she was sober. The possibilities seemed endless.

This was all going on in the fall and I was balancing school, work, and my trips to the cities to see Lora. Every week she grew stronger and more determined. She was to "graduate" and get her medallion in November and Sue and I planned to attend. After that, she was to stay at a halfway house for a limited period of time and then she would be out on her own. Life was finally looking up for her.

Then they told her she had lung cancer. I guess during her physical recovery, Doctor Warren had found a spot on her lung and she went through a series of tests. She had known but didn't want to worry us and besides, she didn't want it to distract her from her recovery. But now they had confirmed it and she was scheduled to go through surgery the day after she completed the program. They were planning to remove two lobes of her left lung and I asked God, "Seriously? Can't you cut her a break? She finally decides to get sober, she leaves the asshole, she's willing to start from scratch to finally get her shit together and this?" However it seemed to affect me, it did not deter her. There was never a moment of self-pity or resentment. It only bolstered her determination. She refused to let it affect her recovery plan and she was determined to go from the hospital to the halfway house. And because she was now sober, she refused any of the pain meds that were prescribed for any patient who underwent this procedure. And although the doctors and even her counselor tried to reason with her, she wouldn't budge and, in fact, went through the post-op recover taking nothing stronger than an aspirin.

She made it through the surgery, went to the halfway house, and was then scheduled to be released. The problem, however, was that she had no place to go. She couldn't return to work for another three weeks. She had no money or even credit to charge things. Until she got her divorce, he still had everything. She asked to extend her stay at the halfway house but they turned her down. She was 48 years old, penniless, and about to be thrown out on the streets, but she was sober. So Sue and I invited her up to the house we were renting in Duluth. I went and got her, packed some of her clothes and drove her up to stay with us. It was fun, actually. I must say I was the only kid at college with his mother crashing at our pad, but other than that it was cool. A lot of our friends got to meet her and as usual, they all loved her and thought I was the luckiest to have her as my mom. And at that moment, I couldn't have agreed more.

Chapter 26

Phill and Sue's Great Adventure

The divorce was pretty quick; very straightforward. She got some furniture and a little cash to get started. We found her a small inexpensive apartment out by the airport. She was back at work and looking forward to starting over. Once she got settled, Susan and I made a pretty monumental decision; we were going to spend six months backpacking throughout Europe with the goal of getting to Greece so I could meet my family.

There was just one problem. Sue lived with her grandmother and finding the money to fund the trip would not be an issue for her. I was broke. My mom was in no position to help and my father spent all of his hard-earned money lavishing him and Barb, and there was never any left over. I knew if he wouldn't help me with college, there was no way he would help fund a trip to Greece. So I dropped out of school, moved back to the city with my mom and went to work at two jobs to earn the money to go. Lora got us jobs at the factory where she worked and I had an ongoing part-time position at a men's clothing store so that's what I did. In fact, that's all I did.

Lora stayed sober for six months. It was the best six months of my life with her and I'm grateful for it. Sue and I were excited to go on our adventure, but after Lora started drinking again I needed to get away. I knew when I got back I would finish college, I just didn't know how or where.

Of course, the trip was fabulous. We traveled around Europe for three months and then when we met my family, they invited both Susan and me to come and work on the island of Rhodes. We ended up spending a year there. We had unbelievable adventures during our year abroad and the trip together really cemented our friendship, love, and trust for each other. We became "friends with benefits." We knew for the rest of our lives we would share memories that were truly our own and although we could share them with family and friends, we knew no one would "get it." We were the only ones and besides, we didn't know anyone who had a similar experience so we always felt as though it was our own. We were even fairly possessive of the whole experience. But eventually September came around again and it was time to go home. Susan had finished school but I still had two years left to get my degree.

The trip was meaningful on so many levels. It was a huge accomplishment; I received zero financial help from anyone. I sacrificed a year of my life working two jobs with practically no free time. But I was determined and I set this as a goal and even though I had no money and no one in my family to turn to, I knew I would do it on my own. It fed my growing confidence that I had what it takes to get what I want in life, without the help of others.

Of course for Susan and me, it was an amazing opportunity to experience being away from the burden of caring for someone at home; for me it was my mom, for her it was her grandmother. This was one of our common bonds; we both understood the burden and the privilege of having to care for a loved one. We could relate to the guilt of wanting to be free to live our own lives and the role of being caretaker. And our friendship and comfort with each other grew stronger. I don't think at that time I had ever been as close to anyone as I was to her.

When we set off to go home, we were looking forward to our future knowing we would hold on to and treasure this part of our past. We were both ready, a year is a long time to be away, especially when you are living in another country. We each had our new goals; mine was to finish college and get my degree, hers was to find a career. We were both moving back home, me with Mom, her with her grandma, but only until I finished school, then we were planning to move in together again because it was familiar to me.

Chapter 27

Starting Over

I came back from living abroad for a year ready to take on the world, even my world, and all that came with it. My family was still not functional, nothing about that had really changed, but it had become easier for me to deal with all of it. We were older, less needy, I was 22 when I came back and enrolled at the University of Minnesota. I was working and paying for school as I went along. To save money I was living with Lora, who by now was in a better place but not great. She was drinking again but not as routinely or severely as before. We actually had a pretty decent apartment with a deck and two bedrooms so she didn't have to sleep on the couch.

Lora had built her own life post-George, and post-Bob. There was new confidence in her and she more or less stabilized. She was still employed and doing well at work. She had established a decent credit rating and even had a little savings. All of this while I was gone. And while there were some occasional drunken binges that were pretty ugly, nothing like before. We settled into a life together, a single mom with her son living at home and going to college. It was mostly very comfortable and this was where her parenting skills were at their best. I didn't need her to take care of me at all; I had a job and paid for my school and for what I needed, so we began to settle into that adult child state of parent and child relationships that we all go through when your children grow up. It was nice, mostly.

Susan continued to be close friends with her and they hung out a lot. She routinely made her semi-famous Sunday Brunch and tons of my friends always showed up and ate and spent the day. I was always so proud of her during these times; I marveled at her abilities to host these events, not just the cooking which was always phenomenal, but her timing, and her ability to be engaging and funny and just how she could work the room. Everyone loved her and so did I.

Everything went pretty well my first year back and I poured myself into my studies. I had completed two years in Duluth and I was determined to finish my degree in four years so that meant taking the maximum allowable credits each quarter plus both summer school sessions while working almost fulltime.

I guess I blame my schedule for not seeing what was happening. I was either working, studying, or in class. We just didn't interact that much and when we did it was usually going out to an occasional lunch or hanging out at one of her ever-popular brunches. Still, I should have seen it coming; after all, I knew her better than anyone.

She had a particularly heavy weekend of drinking, alone, at home. I kind of stayed away with friends, hoping it would blow over. When I came home Monday night after school and work she was already in bed which was unusual but not alarming. I went to bed and woke up the next morning for an early class which meant I had to be out on the road by 6:30 so the fact that I didn't see her wasn't concerning.

When I came home in the afternoon her door was still shut and I began to get this creepy feeling that something was wrong. There were no signs that she had been up, no leftover coffee cup, nothing in the bathroom, everything was just as I had left it.

I walked up to her door and knocked. I slowly opened the door calling out to her. Although it was midday, it was dark in the room as the shades were pulled down and the curtains drawn. She appeared to be sleeping on her back so I went and opened up the curtains to let some light into the room. That's when I knew.

The room was spotless, she was sleeping on top of the bed, not in it, her hair and makeup were perfect and she was wearing a brand-new nightgown. This was her death scene; I knew it because she used to joke about it all the time.

"I think I'd like to be in control of how and when I exit this world. It would be something out of *Kander and Eb.* Probably booze and pills, and of course, they would find me laid out like a queen. Hair in place, perfect makeup, and a lovely new gown."

I didn't rush over to her because I could hear she was breathing, almost snoring; deep low breaths in and out. This time there was no letter, and there was no evidence of what she had done; no empty prescription bottles, no booze, not even an empty glass. The whole scene was so calculated, so well executed, which meant she must have planned it in advance. Once again I was overcome with a lot of conflicting emotions but I wasn't scared, I mean, I didn't know exactly how long she'd been here or specifically when she did it, but if she was still breathing after at least 24 hours, then I figured she'd live through it. I was angry, which made me feel guilty and ashamed, and I was sad. How long had she planned this and why? The fact that it wasn't done in a vengeful and spiteful way made it even more poignant; she actually wanted to spare us all the drama and pain. Why, Mom? I literally stood there and asked her out loud, "Why?"

I slowly and methodically calculated what to do next. I could call the police and an ambulance and I wondered when she woke up what would that would look like. Would she be locked away? Would she lose her job and what little she had struggled to have? Would it mean an end to all that she had worked hard to establish? Was it necessary? How would it help? Right or wrong I made the first decision based on my own assessment of the situation. No calls to the police or a hospital would be made. She did not appear to be in any immediate physical danger and I would not be able to cover up and hide from them what happened. Therefore, this was to remain a secret. I would deal with the problem at hand and once we got through this I would give her an ultimatum; get help or I'm out. Not just moving out, I'm done; I'm burned out, physically, mentally, and emotionally. All of this I would tell her when she woke up, if she woke up. It occurred to me she could be in a coma but that would be a bridge we crossed later, for now I had to take care of the immediate problem.

I walked over and shouted in her face, calling her name and telling her to get up. I got no reaction so I sat on the bed and shook her back and forth, not violently, but enough to wake someone up out a deep sleep. Still nothing. However, I could now see that she had relieved herself all over the bed and was laying on it. This just made me angry and disgusted; once again she got to live her life the way she wanted and I was left to literally clean up the mess she left behind. I wanted to leave her there lying in her own excrements. I wanted to walk out the door and never look back. Instead, I rolled her over and took her things off, removed the dirty sheets, cleaned her up, slipped over an old nightgown and put on fresh linens with two towels and a rubber bath-mat underneath her in case it happened again.

I realize that most people who were suddenly and unexpectedly thrust into this situation may have been panicked and probably would have behaved very differently. I get that. But most people hadn't lived through 22 years of shit that was commonplace in our so-called "family."

When everything was cleaned up and the sheets were in the laundry I went into the kitchen and made some dinner. Then I sat down on the couch in the living room to do homework. I left her door open so I could hear her breathing. There was nothing else to do but wait. If she didn't wake up by morning then she was probably in a coma and I would have to call the police. I wasn't sure exactly what I would say but I'd make something up, I was sure of that, and certainly they couldn't know the truth. As I pondered this potential outcome and the series of events that would inevitably take place I am ashamed to admit that for a moment, just a brief moment, I allowed myself to feel relieved. It would be over and I would be free. I quickly admonished myself for even allowing that kind of thinking and out loud I said to God, "I'm sorry, I'm just tired. Forgive me." Ironically, years later when she did lay there in a coma hooked up to all those machines, I would remember this moment and feel bathed in guilt. But that would be determined in the morning and morning seemed a lifetime away and I was exhausted. As nighttime set in, I fell asleep sitting up with my books everywhere.

"What day is it, how much work have I missed?"

The sound of her voice woke me out of a deep sleep.

"It's Tuesday or maybe Wednesday morning, I don't know what time it is and you've missed two days of work."

"Did they call?"

"Yes, I told them you had intestinal flu and that you would be back as soon as you were sure that you were no longer contagious. They said to take your time."

"Thanks. I'm starving."

"Dinner's on the stove."

"Thanks."

"I'm going to bed, I have early class tomorrow."

"Goodnight, sweetheart."

"Goodnight, Mom. Do not make any plans after work tomorrow and do not have anything to drink. There is a lot I have to tell you and I will need your full and complete attention."

"I figured. I love you."

"I love you too, Mom, but I can't do this anymore."

"I know, neither can I. We'll talk tomorrow."

CHAPTER 28

Out from the Ashes

LORA DID GET HELP. She got a lot of help and worked really hard to get everything together and start to enjoy her life and her talents. She was never lonely, she didn't want a man and she told me that marriage is something you do, with someone you're in love with, to have children. Having been there and done that, she simply saw no point. She had never wanted to marry again and did so only to appease me. She had always been intelligent and independent so living out the rest of her days without the burden of a man suited her just fine.

It was amazing; she pulled herself out from the ashes and began to live life to the fullest, maybe for the first time. Fishing and camping, my mother started going fishing and camping at 51, who knew? These were quiet and peaceful times and as close to normal with her as I'd ever had. I finished school and that fall Susan and I moved into a rented house. I started working full time in retail while Susan had started a career as a travel agent. I planned on taking some time off of school to recharge, earn some money, and then go back for my master's degree.

Everyone, I mean everyone, was proud of Lora, and so happy to see her pull her life together. Few people knew all the sorted details and of course there were even some things that only she and I knew but they all knew enough to know she had had a really rough life. Her best friends ranged from people in their mid-twenties to seniors living out their golden years. At 53, she had hit bottom and was finally coming into her own. This was also significant in that it gave me the freedom I was seeking to pursue my own life goals. It would be a big step for me but I was looking at grad schools in California, and Susan was totally up for our next adventure. Knowing Lora was doing well and could stand on her own gave me the confidence I needed to break away.

Then one night she called me at work, which was unusual even though we talked every day.

"The cancer is back. And this time it's terminal."

Chapter 29

Twilight Zone

Looking back on it, it always seems like one event, as though it was a single occurrence only with different parts. Of course it wasn't, they were two distinctly separate episodes, each occurring a week a part. But whenever I recall it, when I choose to do so, it's all one.

The events leading up to that week, in hindsight, were eerily foretelling, like dialogue written for a movie that foreshadows the impending tragedy for the audience. But at the time, I just shrugged it off, choosing to ignore the real implications of what they both were telling me. Each knew they were going to die—they told me so—I just didn't want to believe them.

Chapter 30

The Last Time . . .

The oncologist gave her roughly six months to live, give or take a month either way. It was lung cancer again. She had never really quit smoking, and more for her comfort than treatment, he recommended she start radiation therapy immediately. Susan and I had just moved into this beautiful home in the suburbs right next door to Susan's best friend from childhood. The owners had bought another even more beautiful home on the lake and we were to live there and maintain it and after a year they would put it back on the market. It was a great deal all around for all of us. They got to have the comfort of not having a house sit empty and a little rent to offset the mortgage; we got to live in a fabulous home with all kinds of space and amenities, like the deck and hot tub, that we otherwise could not have afforded.

So the countdown began. It was fall and soon it would be winter, but there would be no spring. When you lose someone you love to a terminal illness you are keenly aware of the clock ticking and everything is measured as "the last . . ."

The last time we'll have her fall cookout.

The last time we'll celebrate Thanksgiving.

And so on.

Or at least that's how it went for me. It was draining. And she was amazingly strong and stable. It was strange. She said she wasn't afraid of dying, she was afraid of leaving me alone. Nick had his wife and three children, Peter was living with his future wife, and I would be left alone in her mind. In some ways she was right, but not for the reasons she was thinking. It was touching to me that she thought she needed to find someone to watch over me since she would be gone. And in the last years we had grown even closer so I guess I understood that she knew there would be an emotional void for me that would be different from my brothers. She would die, we would all go to her funeral, then my dad and my brothers would go home to their partners and back to their previous lives. I would go home and just be alone. Further, almost all of my life I had taken care of her, been there when she needed me, I was the caregiver, and sadly, I had been the enabler when she was drinking. Burdens, not blessings, but nevertheless, a sense of purpose that would be missing after she died. I wondered, would it be liberating? Would I have a profound sense of relief and freedom or would it be devastating; I've lost my mother and a huge sense of my identity and purpose. These were the thoughts and feelings in my head, and I actually shared them with Susan. We would talk, or rather I would mostly talk and she would listen, but it was so comforting to have her there for me, I was glad they all had their wives but I was very grateful to have my best friend.

I believe gratitude is a choice that God gives to each of us and the blessing is that when your heart and mind are filled with gratitude for all that God has given, there is no room for resentment, fear, loathing, or self-pity. It was hard under the circumstances, but it is, and will always be, my choice. And so I focused on how grateful I was to have these last days with Lora, to be able to plan and say all the things we needed to say to each other. And how grateful to God I was for having Susan in my life and for all my family and friends. I knew that with faith, gratitude, family, and friends, I would be alright.

Chapter 31

But Wait . . .

When Christmas came we all gathered and tried to be jolly. For the most part, it was wonderful, but bittersweet, and I found it hard to accept that this was to be another one of "the last." Lora had moved way out in the country and bought a trailer home just before she was diagnosed with cancer. We all thought it was a stupid and impractical idea but she wanted to own a home of her very own and the truth was, that was all she would ever be able to afford. It was a pain in the ass to drive all the way over but when she got diagnosed and had to start radiation treatments, it became far more than just inconvenient. She was too weak to take care of it so I went out to clean and shovel. In addition, it was winter and a long way from anything, like work, or the clinic, or a hospital. My brothers and I found her an apartment ironically at the same complex she moved to after she and my dad separated. It was cheap and in a great location close to my brother and me. She agreed to sell and move.

Then shortly after Christmas she got really sick. I brought her in to her doctor a couple of times because I was sure she needed to go to the hospital but each time he examined her and said she just needed rest and they sent her home. I blamed it on HMOs and cost containment—in my mind, they were just trying to save money at her expense. I actually got into a confrontation with her doctor on our second visit. The woman was really sick and I assumed that her resiliency was compromised due to her cancer and the treatments, but he was adamant that she just needed some rest so reluctantly I brought her home.

Then she called me again at work, she said she had wet the bed because she literally didn't have the strength to get herself out of bed. I left work telling them, "You can fire my ass but I have to take care of this," and I made the long drive out to her place. When I got there she was really bad and I had to physically carry her out to the car after helping her get changed. I put her in the passenger seat and drove to the doctor. When we got there I was not in the mood for negotiating, I told him to admit her and he said, "Well, that's fine if you want her to have a weekend of rest."

The weekend turned into a week and went on and on. Apparently she developed a case of pneumonia and was expected to recover. But every time I went to see her, which was almost every day, she wasn't getting better. We would walk from her room to go out to the common area and she would have to stop at the nurses' station to catch her breath. She told me that she didn't want to live this way and that if this was the best she was going to get, she would rather be dead.

I assured her that this was temporary and that she was expected to have a full recovery. That's when she said, "I'm never going to leave this hospital, I'm going to die here."

It was weird because I tried to assure her that this would pass but something inside of me told me that she was right. Her oncologists, not the other idiots, told me I was wrong. He explained that her slow recovery was not indicative of her chance for a full recovery. Patients with lung cancer, on radiation, take more time to get over pneumonia. In fact, he said he was very pleased with her overall progress.

So I continued to see her at the hospital in hopes that she would, in fact, recover fully, and we continued to move her stuff into the new apartment. Then one night after I worked a late shift, Susan met me at the door and told me the oncologist called and I was supposed to call him back as soon as I got home. It was about 9:40 at night and I said it was late and that I would call him in the morning but she said he had something really important to tell me and said I should call him no matter what time I got home.

It was a call from heaven. He told me she was responding so well to the radiation that the tumors were, in fact, shrinking. He said he no longer thought the cancer was fast growing and aggressive, but rather, slow growing, and responding well to the treatments. He upgraded his prognosis from six months to "many years." "How many years?" I asked, and he said, "She is not cured of cancer, it is terminal and it will eventually kill her; however, it looks like it will take years to do so, I'd give her ten years at the most." I literally broke down crying, I told him, "Doc, if I ever get diagnosed with terminal cancer, please give me six months and upgrade it to ten years because this is the happiest news you could have told me." I was ecstatic and I told Sue right away and I couldn't wait to call my dad and my brothers in the morning to tell them the news. We had a few drinks and celebrated. I went to bed higher than a kite.

I woke up to intense knocking at my door. Susan was calling my name and telling me to wake up, something about a call from the hospital. It was my day off and I had planned to sleep in. Although I was aggravated at first, I got up and went to the door.

"What, it's my day to sleep in."

"I know but there's a nurse on the phone from the hospital, she says she needs to talk with you, it's urgent."

"Did they say what it's about?"

"No, they will only talk to you. She's on the phone."

"I'll be right there."

I grabbed some clothes and ran upstairs to take the call.

"This is Phill."

"Is this Mr. Williams?"

"Yes, this is Phill Williams, what's the matter?"

"Mr. Williams, you need to come to the hospital right away, it's about your mother, Lora, we have you as the authorized contact."

"Why, what's wrong, is she okay?"

"She's not responding, you need to come down right now."

"What does that mean? Is she all right?"

"All I can tell you over the phone is that she is not responding, I cannot share any other details until you come to the hospital."

"Call my brother Peter."

"We don't have him listed."

"Well, you have me and I am telling you to call him and tell him to meet me there."

I ran upstairs to talk with Susan. I told her about our conversation and she wanted to know what it meant.

"I don't know. She's not responding, I don't know what that means. I think it probably has to do with the antibiotics for her pneumonia, maybe she's spiked a fever and she's not responding to the medications."

"That's probably it, you better get down there, do you want me to come with you?"

"No, I'll call you when I'm there. I'm sure it will be fine."

Chapter 32

The Chaplain

As I pulled into the hospital, my brother was just getting out of his car. We walked together to the lobby and strangely, her oncologist met us in the lobby. I still think this was weird, had he simply been there by coincidence? Otherwise it meant he went down to meet us but he didn't know where we lived or how long it would take us each to get there so that seemed unlikely. Still, there he was waiting in the lobby for us.

We got on the elevator together. The doctor started talking with my brother about her "condition." Tests were being done, something about a brain scan, I tried to follow, but I was distracted by this man who was on the elevator with us. I didn't remember him getting on but he was there and as much as I tried to listen, it bothered me intensely that he was hovering and listening to what should have been a very private conversation. I heard the doctor say something about "not responding" and "we're checking to see the extent of any brain damage."

(BRAIN DAMAGE)

This, of course, caught my attention. I noticed that we passed her floor and I asked the doctor where we were going.

"We had to move her to ICU."

Just as I was going to ask why and what was going on, I couldn't take it anymore and turned to the man and asked, "Sir, can I help you?"

"Actually, I'm here to help you. I'm the chaplain."

(Oh, fuck.)

I don't remember anything the doctor said after that. Whatever it was, it required a chaplain, so clearly this couldn't be good. We got out onto a floor where all the rooms had sliding glass doors with curtains drawn. He walked us to her room and tried to prepare us.

"She seems to be comfortable."

(SEEMS?)

"I warn you, she is hooked up to many life-support machines that provide the functions she needs to live, like breathing, eating, and so forth."

We all walked into the room together. She laid there hooked up to everything as he had warned. I walked over to her, one steel gray eye was open a slit. She was gone.

Just the night before, she was going to dance at my wedding and probably see my children born. Susan and I had celebrated and I was looking forward to being the harbinger of good news in the morning. And then the call, and now everything had changed. This is why faith is so important to me. She had been taken from with without warning, my life for the next ten years, had been taken from me as well. Everything can change. Faith is like integrity, you can lose it, but no one can take it away from you.

When I walked into that hospital room I was in shock. Yet, seeing her only made my faith stronger and more important than ever to me. I prayed for the strength to do the right thing. I knew the decisions would be mine. That's when I made my first of many major decisions; no one was to see her. I refused to have the last memory of her being hooked up to life support. Not this woman who had shown such strength and resilience, she deserved better. I literally collapsed at her bedside. I lay by her and held her hand and put my head on her stomach just as I had when I was a small child.

It sounds so cliché, but it was surreal. I was so unprepared for this, not that anyone could prepare for the literal horror of what happened. She could not breathe on her own, nor could she eat, and she was completely unconscious, but her heart was beating and strong. Every time a nurse came in to check on her they would talk to her, gently, caringly, and I asked why since she was so obviously gone. They told me that they don't know what she can hear so they didn't want to take any chances. I was glad for their care and respect for her, but this was definitely complicating what I initially thought was going to be a difficult, yet single choice to make. From the first moment I saw her, I knew she would never want to live like that. We had seen a television show once where a man had to enter his wife's hospital room with a rifle and threatened to kill anyone who tried to stop him, as he unplugged the machines that were artificially keeping his wife of 50 years alive. My mom said he was a hero, and turned to me and told me that she would count on me to do the same. She literally made me promise.

Her oncologist, all the specialists, told us that it was their belief she would never regain consciousness, based upon all the "tests." I asked what would happen if we continued to provide her with the life support and they said she would remain alive, hooked up to the machines that she was on probably until her heart gave out, which they thought could be a long time.

"There's no brain activity."

(THEN WHY DID YOU TELL US SHE WAS IN A COMA?)

"Her heart is functioning and will continue to do so as long it receives oxygen provided by the ventilator."

(IT'S YOUR "BELIEF" SHE CANNOT RECOVER OR DO YOU KNOW THIS FOR A FACT?)

"Lora, we're going to move your head, we need to wipe up a little blood, it's not serious, it happened when we put the tube in you to breathe."

(YOU DON'T KNOW IF SHE CAN HEAR YOU?)

"Promise me you will never let that happen to me, promise you will never keep me alive on machines."

(I PROMISE, MOM.)

"Hearing may be the last sense we lose."

(THEN I COULD COME HERE EVERY DAY AND TALK TO HER.)

"What do you want to do? This is your decision and we will support whatever want."

(I WANT HER TO WAKE UP.)

Suddenly it wasn't as simple. As I lay there weeping, I held her hand and talked to her hoping the nurses were right, that somewhere down there, wherever she was, she could hear me. Only me, my brother and my dad could see her, and of course Uncle Nick had been told and was flying in from New York. But only us. I mostly just stayed in the room with my head on her while holding her hand. I was aware of the sliding glass door opening and closing and one of them must have come in but I never even looked up to see nor did I know what they did. The only way I knew they had gone was when the door would slide open again. Occasionally some medical staff would have to do something that required me to leave but that was the only time I left the room.

Then late in the day, a nurse came in and said a friend was here and asked to see me.

"No one is to come into the room, I don't want anyone to see her."

"I know that, she didn't ask to come into the room, she asked to see you."

"Where is she?"

"Standing outside the door. You can go into the waiting room if you like, it's just across the hall."

I didn't even ask who it was and I hadn't left her side all day but I thought it would be okay to quickly say hello to whoever it was.

I opened the door and Susan was standing there, still in her winter coat. I collapsed into her arms. We went into the little waiting room. I told her everything. We cried together for a long time. She asked me what I intended to do.

"I don't know, I mean I know what she would want, but what if she could come back? And they talk to her when they're in the room because they don't know if she can hear them. That means I don't know if she can hear me."

She listened and held my hand and we both cried. I said I needed to get back in there to be with her and she got out a paper lunch bag and began showing me what was in it.

"Here, I brought this for you, there's tissues that are soft, not like the cheap hospital kind, your toothbrush and toothpaste because I wasn't sure how long you would be here, and some Snickers bars cuz I know you won't eat but you need to and you love Snickers bars."

(I LOVE YOU. YOU ARE BEAUTIIFUL AND THE BEST FRIEND I HAVE. WHAT WOULD I DO WITHOUT YOU, HOW COULD I EVER GET THROUGH THIS?)

"Thank you, I'm so glad I have you, you know that, don't you? I'll call you later."

"Phill."

"Yeah?"

"I love you too. And I love Lora. What do you think you're going to do?"

"The only real choice I have."

Chapter 33

On the Road to Normal Land

The chaplain turned out to be of great comfort. He listened with wide empathetic (not sympathetic) eyes, and spoke few words, but when he did, they were delivered softly and were mostly meaningful.

He offered to be there with her when they shut down the machines that were artificially keeping her alive. He promised he would not leave her side until she died. When I had informed my family, and the hospital staff, that she was to be taken off all life-support machines, the entire environment changed dramatically. Where prior to this decision, there was quiet, and I was left alone, and people spoke in hushed tones. Now, suddenly there were all kinds of forms to sign and people to talk with. A seemingly never-ending stream of people wanting to discuss details I didn't care to think about. No, I didn't want an autopsy; yes, we want to say goodbye to her in the morning; no, we will not be here to see her unplugged and to watch her die. Yes, I want her cremated. It seemed to go on forever and it became a blur.

Once I had made the decision, I just wanted to go away from this place with the sliding glass doors that required drawn curtains so that no one could see the pain and suffering within. I thought it weirdly appropriate, a metaphor of how I had lived my life. It seemed befitting that my life with my mother would end behind the sliding glass doors with the curtains drawn keeping all the grief and sorrow hidden from everyone.

After we left the hospital Susan and I went home and then out for a few drinks at the neighborhood bar that we loved. We sat for a long time in silence. After a while she asked, "How are you doing?"

"Okay, I guess, considering that tomorrow I'm killing my mother."

"You are not killing Lora. Lora is gone, you know that."

"Yes, I know that. It's just weird, here we are out for drinks, you know, you and I at our favorite local dive bar just like we've done so often, only this time she'll be dead in the morning. Dead, because I made a decision today to stop keeping her alive. I'm having a hard time wrapping my head around the enormity of the situation, what happened today and what will happen tomorrow, juxtaposed against the ordinary, just another night out at the bar, kind of evening we're having."

"Do you want to go home?"

"No, I want to get drunk and not think about my life other than tonight. Tonight, Lora is alive, I still have a mom, and we're together at our favorite bar, and you're here and that's all that matters. See, I can act as if everything is fine."

Susan raised her glass of wine and I raised my bottle of beer.

"To Lora."

"To Lora, and to us. Susan, I don't know how I could have gotten this far without you. You've been here for me and I can't imagine getting through this next chapter without you. Thank you. Don't ever leave me."

Susan smiled back at me and said nothing. Three weeks earlier we had been at this bar sitting in the same booth. I had just come back from visiting Lora and I needed to get out and talk. As always, she was there for me, as I always was for her, and we spent hours talking about Lora and life in general. It was a warm and cozy night watching the snowfall out the windows. I remember feeling almost guilty because I was having such a good time, as though I should only be allowed moments of sadness and grief because my mother was dying of cancer.

I'm not sure if it was the alcohol consumed or the just the buildup of the stress, but at one point I just broke down and gushed, literally, gushed. I was sobbing and slurring about how wonderful she was, how grateful I was to have her friendship, how I could never have gotten through this without her, blah, blah, blah. I was a blithering idiot but she was gracious. It must have been embarrassing for her and I'm sure she got some strange looks from the other patrons who were probably wondering who the moron is with her. At the end of my diatribe, I raised my beer and offered a toast to us, to our seven years of friendship, and to the next fifty years together. That's when she said it:

"There won't be fifty years because I've always known that I will never grow old; in fact, I don't think I have long to live."

She said it as though I was this delicate vase requiring special care and handling so as to not crack or break.

When the day was done I went home to Susan.

Chapter 34

February 10 – February 17

Part 1

So the morning of February 10th we all went to the hospital to say goodbye. The chaplain was there, sitting with her, reading some passages from the bible.

(WE DON'T KNOW WHAT SHE CAN HEAR.)

I thought about whether she knew we were there and that she was scheduled to die and I actually took comfort in that thought. If she could hear, she would want this agony to end. I would be her hero and fulfill my promise.

The chaplain got up and left us alone and we each acted out our grief in our own way. I did not cry; I had no more tears. When we had each said goodbye to this incredible woman, our mother, who had brought us so much pain and joy, I went out to get the chaplain who came in and sat by her bedside. I walked away without looking back, and as I was leaving, somebody brought me a box with her stuff in it: the clothes and jacket she was wearing when she was admitted weeks ago, her reading glasses, books, and piles of her daily crossword puzzles. I don't know why but this really bothered me. I stood in the hall and looked down in the box and didn't move. My dad and my brothers all exchanged looks, not quite knowing how to handle the awkwardness of the moment.

"What the fuck am I supposed to do with this?" I asked her.

"Excuse me?" was her stunned response.

"Why are you giving this to me, I don't want it."

"Sir, we can't keep these things, they don't belong to us."

"They don't belong to me either, they belong to her. She's not even gone yet. She's still here, in that room. Never mind, let's get out of here."

It was a gray, cold winter day and I thought the depressing weather was perfect. It would have really pissed me off if we left the hospital to a bright winter day with blue skies and sunshine. Dad drove out of the parking garage and stopped at the booth where some guy told him he owed two dollars. As my dad fumbled for the cash I just stared at the parking attendant, thinking, *My mother is upstairs dying and you want us to pay for the fucking parking?* Of course, he had no way of knowing, and it was an illogical thought, but it did slap reality right in my face. Take your box, pay your parking tab; life, as they say, goes on.

For the next three days I traveled about with my dad and my brothers doing all these things we had to do. Calls had to be made, forms filled out, there were people and places to see. She died on Thursday and we scheduled her memorial service for Saturday. Never having done this, I was amazed at all the details, the whole thing seemed bizarre to me. When we left the hospital and went to Dad and Barb's, we sat and looked at each other not knowing how one finds a funeral home. In the end, we looked in the Yellow Pages and picked one. I thought, *Really, is this how it's done?* Somehow I had pictured it differently. Later, we were somewhere picking out her urn, like that would matter. I found the whole thing emotionally exhausting and what made matters worse was how *careful* they all were with me. Always asking if I was okay, did I like this or that, was I up for the next thing, and on and on. They treated me as though I was this delicate vase requiring special care and handling so as to not crack or break. I could feel them watching me and I could hear them talk to each other about me in hushed tones when they thought I wasn't listening. Their intentions, of course, were admirable, and I appreciated that they knew this was a different kind of loss for me, but the fact that they thought I could go over the edge really bothered me. Had they only known what I had endured over the years, perhaps they would have realized that I was much stronger than they thought.

However, all the activity and rushing about during the daytime made it easier, the nights when we all went home, were much harder for me. I took great comfort in coming home to Susan. She was my surrogate 'significant other.' They had their wives; I had Susan. We even slept together in the same bed, just two friends, but it helped me feel safe and not so alone.

Part 2

For some reason, I think technically it was her memorial service, and not a funeral, although I'm not sure what the difference is. I had dragged our entourage to the Greek Church and insisted we meet with the priests to make the funeral arrangements. This proved to be an abysmal decision; Father Anthony was a horrible man who made no attempt to hide his disdain for us. We were not members and hadn't attended church, but we were Greek Orthodox and I wanted a religious ceremony. I wrongly assumed we would be greeted with open arms like the prodigal son returning home after years of absence and sin.

I could not have been more mistaken. He sat slumped behind his desk, head resting on his hand and made no attempt to even try to be sympathetic for our loss or act the slightest bit interested. He wasn't even cordial. It was awkward and embarrassing but he agreed to do it, well, not him exactly, he would send Father George, the relic who was his backup but, yes, if we were insisting on a Greek Orthodox funeral it would be done. Thanks, pal.

The service took place in a small and very beautiful byzantine chapel located on the grounds of the cemetery. Susan and I drove to her funeral together. I was so glad to have the time alone to talk about everything. This was it; I was going to my mother's funeral. All the running around and prepping was just rehearsal—this was the final performance. I told her how much it meant to me to have her with me and how it gave me strength to get through this day. When we got there, we were ushered into an adjoining room to wait until everyone had arrived so that the service could get started. We could stay in there or greet and mingle and I chose to stay. I had no desire to talk to anyone. The first three rows were reserved for family. My father turned to Susan and asked her to join us telling her she was one of the family. But she declined, she told him she was honored but since the reception afterward was taking place at the house we rented, she wanted to get out first so that she would have time to make sure everything was set up and ready. She would sit in the back row, closest to the door.

There are things people do that define who they are and this will always be one of those when I think about her. Rather than having the honor of walking up with the family and sitting among us, she wanted to be in the back so she could make sure everything was prepared when all these people came to the house. She had made all the arrangements, everything from the food, to the plates and utensils; she even rented the industrial-sized coffee maker. I didn't have to do anything, she just asked what we wanted and made it happen. She was selfless in that way.

Father George, who had never met Lora, droned on, but he nevertheless read some beautiful passages delivered with warmth and sincerity and words of comfort to us all. And then it was done and just as we were last to be seated we were first to leave. I just walked out without looking at anyone and went to the car.

It was a nice service and a wonderful reception. Friends and family all reminisced about this incredible woman. It was sad but it also filled me with pride. So many people had come to pay their respects and talked so highly of who she was and what she had meant to them. Susan, for the most part, was scurrying around playing the perfect hostess and at one point I literally stopped mid-conversation, excused myself, and grabbed her by the hand and led her upstairs.

I told her everything, everything I had ever wanted to say to her about how much she meant to me, how special she was and how much I loved her. It was completely spontaneous and heartfelt and she stood there crying still holding a coffee pot. Everyone should have that moment with someone they love at least once. It still gives me comfort and I still thank God for that.

As the afternoon turned into early evening, the folks remaining joined us at one of favorite neighborhood pubs for nightcaps. She would have like how the day went. She always wanted an Irish wake. When the evening was over and it was time to go home, I was exhausted. I was glad it was over but also strangely anxious about what was to come next. For three days after she died, there had been a purpose and it occupied our time and left little room for thoughts. Now what? She was gone and there was no more preparation. There were a few things left, insurance, thank-you cards, and the flowers, which had been transported from the chapel to our living room, but mostly it was over. I felt loneliness and fear wash over me. Now it was time to learn to live my life without her. It was like a panic attack coming on and as I sat downstairs looking at the pile of cards and even money I just broke down. I had been solid the whole day; in fact, I never shed a tear but now sitting alone and facing the rest of my life without my mom left me shattered.

I couldn't even bring myself to take comfort in the things she left behind. She had arranged a portrait picture of the two of us so that I could always have it and so that children would see it but now I turned it over not wanting to stir up the memories. The whole room was filled with pictures of her or things that were significant to her like the tennis shoes she had cruelled for me when she got of recovery and was sober for those six glorious months. I know in time I would eventually take great comfort in having all of these, but at that moment they were painful reminders of the void. She was gone.

Susan came downstairs and we sat for a while in the dark. I hadn't slept in my room since that first night we came home from the hospital. I didn't want to be alone but I didn't want to be a burden either. Besides, sooner or later I was going to have to go to my room and start sleeping alone like a grownup. But not yet, she asked me if I wanted to sleep in her room and I gladly accepted. I was going back to work on Monday, so was she, life was going on.

Part 3

The next few days were on autopilot. I was functioning, but not feeling. My brother Nick flew back to New York, Peter and my dad went home and now we all had to go back to our real lives, not the surreal one that the events of the last four days had created. Anyone who has lost a loved one knows, you don't go back to your life because your life has been altered, you go back to life that is different. I think only when you return does the finality and reality begin, and it's not a slow transition, it's a brutal awakening. I guess funerals are probably a good thing; they preoccupy you with all kinds of tasks you need to accomplish. Then there are all the people who pour out their hearts to you about sorry they are, how wonderful she was, and how much they want to be there for you. And they mean that at the time, but of course, most of them won't be. Surprisingly to me, this was far from the worse or hardest part of losing her. I had assumed that the first days having to attend her funeral would be devastating, almost unbearable, and I wondered how I would get through it. I was wrong. The worst part of grieving, the loneliness and sorrow beyond despair, comes after the party, when you're left alone.

I'm not suggesting that my experience was worse, or even different, from anyone else who has gone through the same thing; it was new to me. So, I went to work each day and tried to get back into life, everything was as it was before, I told myself, except she is gone. And at night, I went home and started on the task of writing out thank-you's. I had a stack of cards, some with money, on the coffee table and another stack of thank-you cards with a list of people and addresses. There were probably close to 200 so I figured it would take me a few nights. This was good, I had something to do for a few nights. And then what? I tried not to think about it.

Susan was there and we spent time together every night, but she had a life and I knew it wasn't fair for her to get dragged into what I found myself getting stuck in. She ask if I wanted to go out and meet friends and when I declined she offered to stay in with me but I made her go out. I told her I was fine, just not in the mood, and that spending some time alone was just what I needed. Monday was Valentine's Day and I woke up to find a Miss Piggy card and puzzle from Susan. "Be my tootsie-wootsie or I'll break your armsie-warmsie." It made me smile. We got Muppet humor, we used to get high and watch *The Muppets* at UMD. Back at work for the first time, awkward, but only at the first meeting with my employees or coworkers whom I hadn't seen but obviously knew what had happened. Tuesday and Wednesday, much of the same. Work and then home where I sat and made out cards. Each night Susan would ask me to join her and each night I declined. I'm not even sure why. It's not that I felt sorry for myself but I just couldn't shake the sort of empty feeling. The fact that everyone was expecting me to move on made it harder, it put a kind of self-imposed pressure on me. I felt like everyone was waiting for me to get over it, already, it's been almost a week. And I wanted to but as I said, I felt "stuck." Even the house I came home to was exactly as it was for her funeral reception; cards from the funeral on the table, pictures and memorabilia still displayed and all of the flowers and memorials were still around the house. Somehow I couldn't bring myself to clean up, put things away, and throw out the flowers. I just didn't want to walk to the garbage and throw out the huge heart of roses with the banner that read: "In loving memory of our mother."

Wednesday night when Susan came home she came downstairs and sat by me. I was sitting by the fireplace having just finished all the thank-you cards. She didn't say anything and we both just sat looking at the fire. Then she took a throw pillow from the couch and hit me the face, just out of the blue, without warning. And she hit me hard, I mean it was a pillow, but still. Although it didn't hurt it did startle me and I sort of yelped, "Hey, what was that for?"

She started laughing which made me start laughing. "It's time for you to come back."

"What?"

"No one wants to see you sad."

"I'm not sad, I'm fine."

"Yes, you are and no, you're not."

I just looked at her. She could always read me so well.

"I'm not sure how."

"Well, for one thing you need to get back into your life."

"It's different now."

"Of course it's different now but you are where you are in your own journey and she was a large part of that. Do you think she would want to see you give up? Do you think she would want to see you sad?"

"No."

"And Phill, go ahead and feel it, all of it, this is not something you'll be able bury. Don't be afraid."

"I'm not afraid."

"Yes, you are."

"Alright, I'm afraid. But what happens if I just open that up and let all those thoughts and feeling flood in, what if I can't, you know, get back?"

"Get back from where?"

"From wherever it takes me."

"Well, I'm here, I'll be here to help you. You'll be fine."

I turned back to the fire and thought for a while about what she had said. She was right. Lora would never have wanted me to be sad and depressed. I had to find gratitude for what God had given me, not resentment for what I lost. I suddenly felt energized, like a veil had been lifted and I could see clearly. I jumped up and turned on the light.

"Okay, Scott and Brenda called and they wanted to stop by so I'll invite them over for tomorrow night and we can have a few drinks. We haven't seen them for a long time, it will be fun to get together."

"Sounds great. I'll invite Patty."

"Yes, do invite Patty, I'd love to see her."

"I have Friday off so I'm going to mail all these thank-you cards and put all this stuff away."

"Sounds like a good plan. What about the flowers?"

"I'll throw them away, I'm ready."

"Great."

"Except, Sue, could you do me a favor? Would you take the big one for Mom and get rid of it somewhere, like not in our garbage? I just don't want to see it in our trash."

"I understand, I'll take care of it on Friday while you're cleaning up and putting things away."

"Thank you."

"Coming to bed?"

"Can I, just one more night, I promise."

"You can stay with me as long as it takes you to get back on your feet."

"Thank you, I'm ready. Just one night more."

Thursday, February 17th, exactly one week after Lora died. I knew the moment I woke up that this was going to be a much better day. It felt different. It wasn't that I suddenly had no sadness or that I was over the grieving—far from it—I just had a plan. One day at a time. Today, I was going to work and I would redo the displays, spring was around the corner and we needed something to brighten up the cold and dreary February days. After work we were entertaining friends, and I was actually looking forward to it. It's weird, but I kind of had this feeling that enjoying myself would somehow minimize or trivialize my loss. It didn't and I was coming to accept that it was simply part of going forward, just as she would have wanted. I was strong, and I had support. It was okay to have fun again.

When I came home it was much better and I think Susan and Kent, our friend and roommate, could sense it. Talk was brighter, we laughed more openly, and it just felt much more like "back to normal." While we waited for our friends to come over, I went downstairs to take some time looking over everything. I was ready, I actually wanted to get started that night. It was weird, just the day before I could hardly bring myself to think about taking it all down and getting the house back to its pre-funeral reception state. Now suddenly I was anxious to get rid of all of it, it seemed depressing and morose. But I guess that says a lot about where my head was at during that first week. Enough. I knew I wasn't over sadness but it was time to get my life moving forward again. I even went through the photos and other special things that were just about her and me and it didn't make me sad, or at least it didn't make me cry.

So they all came over and we sat and had a few drinks and a good time. Good company, good conversation, and good friends: exactly what I needed. I had a couple of beers and Kent drank a few shots but no one got drunk or disorderly. It was actually pretty low key. Later, during the investigation and litigation, much would be made of the vodka bottle that Kent left out on the kitchen counter, leading to speculation, and accusations, that a drunken brawl had taken place that night, culminating with an orgy in the hot tub, but this was simply not true. It was a quiet, fun, small get-together.

We used the hot tub frequently that winter. It required some planning as you had to turn the heat up to get it ready and that took a couple of hours. That night, we all planned to go in the hot tub, but by the end of the evening I was too tired and only Susan and Kent donned their bathing suits and grabbed their towels to face the bitter cold first few steps in the snow before the amazing heat of the water and the soothing jets. We would often go in the hot tub late at night, just before bed, because it always made you relaxed and ready for sleep. We used to joke that it was the best sleeping aid ever. And the combination of alcohol and the hot tub was almost like a drug; you knew you would fall into an instant and heavy sleep. Looking back I have often wondered if I had gone with them in the hot tub, if that somehow would have changed what happened. I couldn't help thinking that perhaps that was why they didn't wake up earlier. And if that was true, why didn't I go with them? I changed my mind at the last minute. But these were just a few of the things that happened that night that I have rerun in my head over and over again searching for answers that can never be found.

When they finished, Kent helped clean up and he took the ashtrays out to the garage, something we always did as a precaution. Susan went up and changed into her goofy flannel nightgown and came back downstairs wrapped in her enormous floor-length blue robe. At only twenty-eight, she managed to pull off a middle-aged matron look better than a 50-year-old and I often teased her about it.

"Coming to bed?"

"Yeah, I'm beat, this was fun, thank you."

"For what?"

"For hitting me in the face with what I assume was a sack of potatoes."

She started laughing, that wonderful, contagious laughter that only came from her.

"Those were not potatoes, they were bricks."

"Gee, thanks. Whatever it was, it managed to knock me out of my slump."

"I'm glad. So big day tomorrow, you're ready to take all this down?"

"Yes, I'd do it tonight if I had the energy."

She turned to go upstairs. "Coming up?"

"No, I'm fine. Time to go bed, in my own bed, in my own room."

Susan smiled at me, like a proud parent who was just handed a picture their kid made at school. "Nice to have you back. Oh, and Phill, I'll take the wreath out tomorrow when I come home for lunch. Goodnight."

"Goodnight, Sue, see you tomorrow."

Chapter 35

Hello – Goodbye

I COULD NOT SEE WHO WOKE ME UP out of a sound sleep. I had no idea what time it was but the room was dark and I figured it was still the middle of the night. I pulled down the covers and sat straight up.

"Hello?"

No answer. I sat on the edge of the bed and waited for my eyes to adjust to the darkness. No one was there. Whoever had woken me up must have gone out and I figured maybe they were waiting outside my door. I had the room in the basement. The house was a multi-level split so there were center stairs that took you to the main floor and kitchen then upstairs to the bedrooms where Susan and Kent slept. My bedroom was actually part of a small mother-in-law's mini apartment and it was just off the downstairs family room where we had all been earlier. My bedroom door opened into the little apartment and through there you could go the left where the door opened to the family room or to the right where you walked out to get to the hot tub.

I sat on the bed and looked at the door. I called again but no one answered. I was actually irritated and I considered just going back to sleep but I had this weird feeling that someone was standing right outside my door in the apartment, a feeling I couldn't shake. So, I got out of bed and grabbed a shirt off the floor and walked to the door. Then I stopped. To this day I cannot explain it, but it was as if someone were calling me to come to them, but not with words. I stopped because I expected to see someone waiting for me on the other side of the door. Again, I debated my next move; chase after this strange feeling or do the logical thing and just go back to bed. I opened the door and stepped out.

The flames were covering the ceiling and coming down the walls. They enveloped the curtains and the outside of my bedroom door. There was no sound and there was no air as though the fire was consuming everything. I stood in middle of the room, not moving. As I looked to my left I could see into the family room, the door was gone and in there the fire completely raged so that all you could see was a wall of flames from floor to ceiling; it reminded me of when I was a kid and I would go downstairs in the winter and peek through the window into the incinerator where they burned our trash; nothing but flames of raging fire.

Still, I didn't move. Somehow, I couldn't; my mind literally could not grasp what was happening. I stood still taking it all in, trying to make sense of it. Then in an instant I snapped out of my daze and it all became crystal clear. I realized immediately that this was real, this was no fucking dream; the house is on fire and I'm going to die if I don't get out. And so will Susan.

I was competing with the fire for oxygen and losing, I could hardly breathe, the air was hot and toxic. I turned to my right to get to the door that led outside to the patio and hot tub. My hands were shaking uncontrollably as I grabbed the handle to open the door. The door wouldn't budge. Panic and bile came gurgling up my throat and I started to pound at the door turning the handle left and right over and over while pulling to jar it lose. I could feel the heat of the fire and it felt like the flames were coming closer and growing larger. Then the door finally came open but there was a storm door so I had one more barrier to break through to get out of the burning house. It opened with surprising ease and when it did I was literally thrown out the door, as though the house was ejecting me, and I landed in the deep snow on my hands and knees. I sat there shaking, gasping for air and taking great gulps of breaths over and over. I was out, but Susan was still in.

CHAPTER 36

Hello – Goodbye, Part II

O*WE'VE ALL HAD THAT DREAM*. The names change, and the circumstances may be different, but fundamentally it's the same nightmare. You're in danger and you try to run but your feet are heavy and you can't seem to get them to move quickly or cooperate so the imminent menace is getting closer and closer. Still, you try even harder, you know you must get away but the harder you try the slower you go. And then you are screaming but nothing comes out, you can't make a sound and the terror builds inside of you, your heart pounding, you are practically paralyzed with fear. It's getting closer and closer and you can't get away. And then it is upon you.

And you wake up in a cold sweat.

I was absolutely crazed with panic and fear. The house was on fire; this was real. I had no idea how bad the fire was throughout the house. I knew I had to wake up Susan so she could get out. I lifted my head and could see her bathroom window. It was dark and there were no signs of the fire upstairs.

I stood up in the deep snow and started to pound on the side of the house screaming. I had to wake her up; I had to get her out. I knew it was all up to me, whether she lived or died would depend on me. At least that's how it felt. Nothing else mattered, I was outside in the snow, in subzero temperature wearing only a shirt, and I didn't even notice the cold. I started to make my way around to the house where her bedroom was, and the front door, screaming for her to wake up and get out of the house. With each second, I became more panicked, but the harder I tried to go, the slower I went, just like the dream.

It was the snow. There were 25 inches of snow on the ground in our backyard. I know that because from the ground to my mid-thigh is 25 inches and that's where the snow came up to on me. But there was also a thin layer of ice and, because of the ice, I could walk on top of the snow a few steps until my bare feet broke through the layer and I was once again trudging through snow up to my thighs. I was struggling with great effort and only able to move a few inches—the shattered ice cutting my feet and leaving a trail of blood. Then I would start all over pulling myself out of the snow and trying to move as quickly as I could.

When I finally got to the front yard it was much better because the snow was harder and packed down. As I came around the corner I looked up to her window, still screaming for her to get out of the house. Nothing. Her room was dark and I could see the white curtains tied back in place so it didn't appear the fire had reached the upstairs. But there was nothing in the windows, it was eerily dark, and still.

Then I heard this awful sound coming from the front of the house in the entryway. It was horrible. It was high pitched and staccato and it sounded like an animal. I knew it was coming from the other side of the front door so I ran to open it hoping it was Susan. I didn't stop to think about how I would get the door open, of course it was locked and I certainly did not have a key on me; nevertheless, I ran to open it, the horrible screaming getting louder and louder. When I grabbed the handle it turned easily and I threw open the front door.

Kent came running out. I had completely forgotten about Kent. He ran past me and dove into the snowbank. Every second of that night is indelibly cast in my brain forever but that particular moment is especially clear. I can never forget what it looked like, what it sounded like, what it felt like, or what it smelled like. The high-pitched, animal-like shrieking, the intense heat and smothering toxic smoke that blasted through the doorway when I opened it. Kent was screaming because he was trapped in the entryway. He had managed to turn the handle, which, thank God, popped the lock, but the handle burned his hand and he couldn't get the door open. He was trapped in the dark, in the smoke, and in the burning house. When he ran past me he was on fire. You never forget the smell of smoke and burning flesh.

I stood holding the door open, the thick, toxic smoke and heat pouring out of the open door. I was screaming for Susan, I assumed she would be right behind Kent but she wasn't. I wanted to run inside and find her but the heat and smoke were overpowering. When it was clear she wasn't there I shut the door and ran over to check on Kent. He was groaning in the snow and barely conscious, but he was breathing. I asked him if he saw Susan, if he knew where she was or what happened to her but he said he never saw her. I had to get help. Kent needed to get to a hospital and Susan was either dead or trapped somewhere in the house.

Chapter 37

The Sirens, the Ambulance, and the Chaplain

I *RAN NEXT DOOR TO OUR FRIEND'S HOUSE* and banged on their door. When they opened their door I went inside and collapsed on their floor. My hair, and even my eye lashes, were burned off and I must have looked like I escaped from an asylum.

"The house is on fire."

"Get in, oh my God."

"No, Susan, she's still in there. I can't find her. She's still in the house, I have to get her out."

"Oh my God, Bob, call 911."

"Tell them she's in there. Tell them that. They have to get here right away. Where is she? She's not in her room; she didn't come out with Kent."

"So Kent is out?"

"Yes, but he's hurt bad, he has to get to a hospital. I'm going back to find Susan."

They tried to stop me but I went anyway. I ran back to the house and Kent was coherent and I was able to talk to him.

"Hold on, Kent, we've called 911, help is on the way."

"Susan."

"I know. We'll get her out."

"No, she's there, I was talking to her."

My heart just about jumped out of my chest, I had honestly thought she was dead. I ran to the front and there was a heavy stream of black smoke billowing out her window, it was so thick that at first I didn't see her so I called out to her. She was there, her face pressed up against the screen so she must have been on her knees. Her bedroom was on the second floor and she had a large picture window with two smaller windows that opened on each side. And that's where she was. It was too far up for me, or anyone, to reach but not so high that she couldn't jump down. She had managed to unlatch the lock and push up the window but not the screen.

"Susan, you're here. My God, I was so scared, I couldn't find you."

"I can't get out."

"Open the screen."

"I can't."

"Break the window."

"I can't."

"Susan, listen to me, next to you just on your left is a small table; pick it up and throw it through the window."

"I can't. I can't move, I can't see anything."

"Okay, don't move. Just stay where you are. We've called the police and the fire department, they'll be here any second."

"I'm not going to make it."

"Susan, please, I can hear the sirens, see, they're coming. You can hear them, can't you? You have to hold on."

"I can't breathe. . . I'm going to die in here."

"SUSAN, NO! Please, don't panic, they're on their way. You have to hold on. Look, I can hear the sirens; they're getting closer. They're almost here. Can't you hear them? Please, hold on."

"I can't hold on."

I saw her drop. I heard her hit the floor. I watched her die in front of me; she trapped inside a burning house, and me, outside and safe, completely unable to save her. I'd never felt so helpless or worthless.

Then a policeman was there in my face and I was banging on his chest and yelling at him to help me go in and get her out. I told him I know where she is. But he just took me away to our friend's house and told them to wait with me until the ambulance came. When they got me in the ambulance, I asked if they got Susan out and they said they did but they wouldn't tell me how she was, only that she was being taken to the hospital. It gave me hope even though I knew better. Maybe I was wrong, maybe she wasn't dead and they would save her. This guy in a white uniform put an oxygen mask on me and was asking me questions, did I know what day it is, and what year. They were stupid questions and it was hard to talk clearly with the mask on but when I went to take it off he wouldn't let me. There was another man in the ambulance with us who was not wearing a uniform. He had dark hair and a beard and he was down toward the end of my stretcher. He reached up and took my hand.

"Phill, I'm the chaplain."

"Oh, fuck."

Chapter 38

There Are No Words

KENT WAS RUSHED IMMEDIATELY UP TO SURGERY but I was put in a stall in the ER and so was Susan. I could hear them working on her, I could their voices and the sound of medical devices. One must have been for breathing because it was rhythmic and even, in and out, just as my mother's had been. I lay on the table hooked up to oxygen while they examined me and all the while, I just kept asking about Susan.

And then it got quiet. No sounds from the stall next to me. I knew she was dead, I knew before the chaplain came in and took my hand, with his sad eyes and gentle caring voice. Poor guy had to break the news to me and I thought about how often he had to do this and why anyone would want his job. I just stared at him. And that's when I went away again just like I had done when I was a kid and I saw my mom. I was there but I wasn't there.

Mom was gone, Susan was gone, my home and everything I owned were gone. Just a week ago, I had a different life. I wasn't married but I lived with my closest friend and we had our life together. I didn't own a house but I had a home. I was Lora's son, taking care of her was a blessing and it was a burden, depending on the day, but either way, it was definitely part of my identity. Now in one week, my life, as I knew it, was gone. Had it not been for my unfaltering faith I don't know how I could have kept going. Perhaps others have strength I lack, but seriously, my deep imbedded faith in God seemed to me, at the time, all that I had left, and all that I needed, to get through this and move forward.

Susan's funeral was on the following Monday. The week before, we had gone together to my mother's funeral but this week, I would go alone to hers.

CHAPTER 39

Baggage

post-trau·mat·ic stress dis·or·der
noun: **post-traumatic stress disorder:**
a condition of persistent mental and emotional stress occurring as a result of injury or severe psychological shock, typically involving disturbance of sleep and constant vivid recall of the experience, with dulled responses to others and to the outside world.

Survivor guilt (or **survivor's guilt**; also called **survivor** syndrome or **survivor's** syndrome) is a mental condition that occurs when a person perceives themselves to have done wrong by surviving a traumatic event when others did not.

I *HAVE READ ABOUT* Post-Traumatic Stress Disorder and "survivors guilt," and I believe them to be real. It's hard to explain what those days, and months, following that week were like. The fire scene would play in mind without warning, the scene started when I woke up and ran completely until they put me in the ambulance. It was vivid and frightening because initially I couldn't control it, like someone had pushed the play button and I couldn't stop it or even pause it. I would be driving on the highway and suddenly I was there again, back at that night, and when it was done I would look out to see that I had driven miles past my exit. And I never again slept through the night, to this day I haven't. I wake up several times in the night out of a deep sleep, and I am completely awake and aware of my surroundings. Once I see that everything is fine, I fall immediately back to sleep.

But the guilt was by far the worst part of my life at that time. It was overpowering and seemed insurmountable. I would literally be crushed by feelings of remorse and shame. George Erickson was the fire chief and he told me how lucky I was, he said that had I slept another 20 minutes, I would have simply died in my sleep and never woke up. He said based on the location of the fire and the proximity to my room, "You are lucky, you should have been the first to go." Never, did I ever, feel fortunate. I felt like shit.

There were so many complicating factors. I was supposed to get her out. I got out, and she had to spend the last minutes of her life knowing I was out, and safe, while she knew she was going to die trapped in the house. Then there was Kent. I saved his life but I never meant to. I was so singularly focused on getting Susan out that night that I never even thought about Kent. And finally, I thought I may have started the fire. I had this terrifying fear that I forgot to blow out a candle that I had lit by the TV, the very area we all knew was where the fire started. So in my mind, not only did I fail her, I might have killed her as well.

Of course, I told no one. Never one to talk about my feelings, I didn't know how to go about it. I just wanted to get the grieving process over with; that's how ignorant I was. So I tried attending a support group. The chaplain from North Memorial Hospital had given me a card for a person who headed a grief support group that met weekly at the hospital. Susan's best friend Patty, and the neighbor whose house I had gone to that night, went with me to a meeting. It wasn't what I had expected; it was like a scene from the old *Bob Newhart* show. They all seemed to know each other and as folks came in it was like a social gathering with each of them catching up with one another regarding the significant events since their meeting the previous week. Then there was the rocker, the knitter, and the nodder. One man rocked constantly back and forth, the knitter was a woman who never stopped knitting, the clicking of her needles was relentless, and the nodder shook his head as if in violent agreement with everything anyone said. And no one seemed to notice or find this unusual, but me. So the meeting began and Carl the leader introduces himself and provides a brief description of why we were all here and then he points out that there are two new people and explains to us, apparently as tradition dictates, that we go around the room while each person explains why they are here and what loved one they lost, and that's how the meetings begin.

So everyone introduces themselves and shares their story. The first thing that I notice is that most of the people there had lost someone a long time ago. It bothered me to think that I might still need to come to a grief support group for months, or in some cases years. Always a fast learner and overachiever, I assumed I could get through the whole grieving process quickly and then get on with building a new life. That's why I had agreed to come this support group in the first place, I assumed it would speed things up. Now that I was there, I was sitting with people who have been coming every week for the last year or two, which was quite discouraging.

After everyone was done it was my turn, as a new member, to share why I was there. Now you have to understand that this was a very somber atmosphere, as you can imagine. It was, after all, a support group for people grieving the loss of loved ones. But for some reason, I found it funny, which was horrifying and completely inappropriate, like laughing out loud in church. So leader Carl asks me to introduce myself and to tell the group about my loss. And so I told them about Lora and all the while everyone was looking at me with great sympathy and understanding, the room hushed but for the constant clicking of the knitting needles. The rocker rocked and I thought the nodder was going to get whiplash. When I finished telling them about my mother's death, which had occurred less than two weeks prior, there was this sort of moment of silence, which made me uncomfortable but they all seem to have this thing down so I just did what they did. Then the leader Carl looked somberly at me and said in a quiet and calming voice,

"Thank you for sharing your story, Phill. We can all appreciate the pain and suffering you must be experiencing. We've all been there and we're here to help."

"Thank you, Carl."

"No, thank you for coming tonight and sharing." Then he turns to Patty and says, "And you are?"

"Excuse me, Carl."

"Yes, what is it, Phill?"

"I'm not done yet."

"Phill, first we let everyone share their story, you'll have a chance to talk more when we're done." He turns back to Patty.

"Carl."

"Yes, Phill?"

"I'm not done sharing my story."

"But you told us about your mother's illness and death."

"I know, that was on the 10th, then a week later . . . ."

Had awards been handed out that night I would have gone home with the biggest prize. They sat stunned as I then told them what happened the following week. They might as well have bowed their heads down and chanted, "We are not worthy." It's probably just me, but it seemed like they were genuinely impressed. I knew then that I wasn't ready for a support group. While the first round of silence and sympathy upon hearing of my mother's demise had been generously poured out, the second round was even more lavish and it literally stopped the meeting, even the clicking of the knitting needles halted momentarily. When I finished, virtually everyone felt compelled to express their condolences. I felt sorry for Patty, mine was obviously a tough act to follow.

Rather than seek an alternative therapy to help me get through the sleepless nights, random panic attacks, and general depression, I, of course, chose to not seek any professional help. Instead, I focused on my spiritual needs and to that end, I began meeting with Gary, a protestant pastor that Patty introduced me to. By now I had developed a general fear and distrust for chaplain-like people but Gary turned out to be okay and, while I didn't meet with him for very long, he nevertheless helped me to focus my faith and helped to me trust my life in the hands of God. It was reinforcement to what I already knew but during that time of my life, I needed validation.

Kent survived and spent months in rehabilitation. A forensic report came back from Texas with conclusive evidence that faulty wiring in the new television had caused the fire. This, of course, was a huge weight of guilt lifted off my shoulders. I still had to live the rest of my life knowing I failed to save

Susan because I made so many mistakes, but at least I hadn't been responsible for the fire that killed her.

When the summer came I found a place to live with Kent. It was a sad time in my life. I just sort of functioned. The tape continued to play randomly in my head and for a long time, I would recount all the mistakes I made that led to Susan's death. There was no working smoke detector, I should have quietly gone to the front of the house and tapped on Susan's side bedroom window, which I could have reached if I had stepped up onto the brick ledge. Had she not opened the door she would not have let all the toxic smoke in that killed. Her deadliest mistake was opening the window after she opened her bedroom door. This created a vacuum effect that sucked all the smoke in the burning house up to her room and out her window where she was trying to get air.

But she no doubt opened her door because she heard me screaming to get out. And then there was Kent, so grateful, telling me repeatedly how thankful he was that I had saved his life and all I could think was that I never meant to, I was trying to get Susan out.

I missed my mom, I missed Susan, I missed my things. It wasn't so much my clothes or furniture or those material things as much as all of the sentimental things. Pictures, gifts from my mom, you know all the stuff that has no value to anyone else, but you cherish them for the memories just the same.

I was 25 and it was exactly one year before I would meet my wife. Normal was sounding better than ever to me. In my own way, I could still find gratitude. My life experiences leading up to that week had certainly prepared me to withstand the emotional trauma. I wanted a life again. And I wanted more than ever what I had always wanted; security and safety and happiness. I believed that a family would give me all of that. And perhaps more important, I didn't think I could get the things I wanted and needed anywhere else. I wanted a sense of purpose and I wanted to make up for all that I had done or not done to save Susan. I wanted a family of my own desperately. I knew I could take care of my family, I was trained from early childhood to be responsible, and to provide, and take care of someone. Knowing that someone was out there, and that I just had to find her, gave me hope and made this horrible "in-between" time in my life more bearable. I turned 26 that summer, I had a new job and a great career ahead of me. I was a good catch, all I needed to do was keep all the baggage and emotional damage hidden away. I had to act "as if" I was just another normal average Joe, which I knew I could do—I'd been faking that all my life. In my ignorance, I believed that I could suppress the trauma and pain and not suffer any side-effects. Of course, I was wrong.

Twenty years later when I finally accepted the truth about my sexual orientation, it was, in fact, tremendously liberating. Almost from the moment I stopped trying to fight it, I was changed—more confident, less angry, more at peace. However, the journey to get there was very difficult, emotionally, psychologically, and even physically. There were a lot of conflicting emotions: fear, shame, guilt, and sadly even despair. I thought it was so unfair, I just wanted to be normal, like everyone else. Coming to terms with my sexual orientation and admitting that I was a homosexual took strength and courage that I didn't have back then. I needed to recover not just from the fire but from the cumulative effects of everything that had shaped the first quarter of a century of my life. At that time, I was trying to figure out how to make it through the day, I had to rebuild my life and I didn't have the wherewithal to throw on top of it, "Why not check out this gay thing and see where that takes me?" What I wanted and needed most was stability. I wanted the family I had never had, and I wanted to provide my children with everything I felt I had been denied.

And I needed to deal with all the things I had locked away. All my life I had held in all of my fears, keeping them a secret to the outside world. Don't let anyone know what goes on in your family or what kind of freak you are. No one will accept you and no one will love you. However hard you try or how successful you are at keeping it all inside, eventually if you don't deal with these things they will manifest themselves in some other ways. Of that I am convinced because that is what happened to me. Some people become physically sick, others might battle depression. For me, these tools or rather weapons for survival, led to almost uncontrollable anger and rage and isolation. As I got older, it was not possible for me to have intimacy because I didn't know how. I had become a control freak and the only emotion that I registered easily was anger.